JOSEPH
STALIN

———•—★—•———

A Short Biography

COMPILED

by

G. F. Alexandrov, M. R. Galaktionov,
V. S. Kruzhkov, M. B. Mitin,
V. D. Mochalov, P. N. Pospelov.

University Press of the Pacific
Honolulu, Hawaii

Joseph Stalin:
A Short Biography

Compiled by
G. F. Alexandrov
M. R. Galaktionov
V. S. Kruzhkov
M. B. Mitin
V. D. Mochalov
P. N. Pospelov

ISBN: 1-4102-0431-6

Reprinted from the 1950 edition

University Press of the Pacific
Honolulu, Hawaii
http://www.universitypressofthepacific.com

I

JOSEPH VISSARIONOVICH STALIN (DJUGA-SHVILI) was born on December 21, 1879, in the town of Gori, Province of Tiflis. His father, Vissarion Ivanovich Djugashvili, a Georgian of peasant stock from the village of Didi-Lilo in the same province, was a cobbler by trade, and later a worker at the Adelkhanov Shoe Factory in Tiflis. His mother, Ekaterina Georgievna, was born of a peasant serf named Geladze, in the village of Gambareuli.

In the autumn of 1888 Stalin entered the clerical school in Gori, from which, in 1894, he passed to the Orthodox Theological Seminary in Tiflis.

This was a period when, with the development of industrial capitalism and the growth of the working-class movement, Marxism had begun to spread widely through Russia. The St. Petersburg League of Struggle for the Emancipation of the Working Class, founded and led by Lenin, gave a powerful impetus to the development of the Social-Democratic movement all over the country. The tide of the labour movement swept as far as Transcaucasia, where capitalism had already taken a foothold, and where the burden of national and colonial oppression weighed

5

heavily. An economically backward, agrarian country, where survivals of feudalism were still strong, and where numerous nationalities lived intermingled together, Transcaucasia was a typical tsarist colony.

In the last quarter of the nineteenth century, capitalism had begun to develop rapidly in Transcaucasia, savagely exploiting the workers and peasants and aggravating the national and colonial yoke. Particularly rapid was the development of the mining and oil extracting and refining industries, the key positions in which had been seized by foreign capital. "Russian capitalism," wrote Lenin, "drew the Caucasus into the sphere of world commodity circulation, obliterated its local peculiarities—the remnants of ancient patriarchal isolation—and *created for itself a market* for its goods. A country which was thinly populated at the beginning of the post-Reform epoch, or populated by mountaineers who lived out of the course of world economy and even out of the course of history, was being transformed into a land of oil operators, wine merchants, big wheat growers and tobacco growers...."* The appearance of railways and of the first industrial plants in the Caucasus was accompanied by the appearance of a working class. Especially rapid was the development of

* V. I. Lenin, *Collected Works*, 3rd Russ. ed., Vol. III, p. 464.

J.V. STALIN
Photo 1894

the oil city of Baku, a big industrial and working-class centre in the Caucasus.

As industrial capitalism developed, the working-class movement grew. In the 'nineties revolutionary activities in Transcaucasia were carried on by Russian Marxists who had been exiled to that region. The propaganda of Marxism began in Transcaucasia. The Tiflis Orthodox Seminary at that time was a centre from which libertarian ideas of every kind spread among the youth—from nationalist Narodism to internationalist Marxism. It was honeycombed with secret circles of various descriptions. The jesuitical regime that reigned in the seminary aroused in Stalin a burning sense of protest and nourished and strengthened his revolutionary sentiments. At the age of fifteen Stalin became a revolutionary.

"I joined the revolutionary movement," Stalin says, "at the age of fifteen, when I established connection with certain underground groups of Russian Marxists then living in Transcaucasia. These groups exerted a great influence on me and instilled in me a taste for illegal Marxian literature."[*]

In 1896 and 1897, Stalin led Marxist study circles in the seminary, and in August 1898 he formally enrolled as a member of the Tiflis organization of the Russian Social-Democratic Labour Party. He joined the first Georgian Social-Democratic organization,

---

[*] J. V. Stalin, *Interview with the German Writer, Emil Ludwig*, Russ. ed., 1938, p. 9.

known as the Messameh Dassy. This group, in the years 1893-98, performed a certain useful role in the propagation of Marxist ideas. But it was not a politically homogeneous organization. The majority of its members shared the views of the "Legal Marxists" and inclined towards bourgeois nationalism. Stalin, together with Ketskhoveli and Tsulukidze, formed the leading nucleus of a revolutionary Marxist minority in the Messameh Dassy, from which sprang the revolutionary Social-Democratic movement in Georgia.

Stalin worked hard to broaden his knowledge. He studied *Capital,* the *Communist Manifesto* and other works of Marx and Engels. He acquainted himself with Lenin's writings against Narodism, "Legal Marxism" and "Economism." Even at this early date Lenin's writings made a deep impression on him. "I must meet him at all costs," one of Stalin's close friends of that time reports him to have said after reading an article by Tulin (Lenin).*

Stalin's range of theoretical interests was extremely broad. He studied philosophy, political economy, history and natural science. He read widely in the literary classics. Stalin became an educated Marxist.

At this period Stalin carried on intense propaganda in workingmen's study circles, attended illegal

* Reminiscences of Com. P. Kapanadze, in *Recitals of Old Transcaucasion Workers About the Great Stalin,* Russ. ed., Young Guard Publishing House, 1937, p. 26.

workers' meetings, wrote leaflets and organized strikes. It was among the advanced proletarians of Tiflis that Stalin got his first schooling in practical revolutionary work.

"I recall the year 1898," Stalin later said,* "when I was first put in charge of a study circle of workers from the railway shops.... It was here, among these comrades, that I received my first revolutionary baptism ... my first teachers were the workers of Tiflis."

The program of the workingmen's Marxist study circles in Tiflis was compiled by Stalin.

The seminary authorities, who kept a strict watch on "suspects," began to get wind of Stalin's secret revolutionary activities, and on May 29, 1899, he was expelled from the seminary for Marxist propaganda. For a time he lived by giving lessons; later (December 1899) he found employment at the Tiflis Physical Observatory as a calculator and observer. But never for a moment did he cease his revolutionary activities.

Stalin had now become one of the most active and prominent members in the Tiflis Social-Democratic organization. "In 1898-1900 a leading, central Social-Democratic group of the Tiflis organization arose and took shape.... The central Social-Democratic group of Tiflis did an enormous amount of

---

* J. V. Stalin, *Collected Works*, Russ. ed., Vol. 8, p. 174

revolutionary propagandist and organizational work for the formation of an illegal Social-Democratic Party organization."* This group was headed by Stalin. Lenin's League of Struggle for the Emancipation of the Working Class was the model on which the revolutionary Social-Democrats of Tiflis faithfully moulded their activities. At this period the labour movement in Tiflis, led by the revolutionary minority of the Messameh Dassy (Stalin, Ketskhoveli and Tsulukidze), ceased to confine itself to the old, purely propaganda work for "outstanding individuals" among the workers; the prime task, dictated by developments, was now mass agitation, by means of leaflets on burning questions of the day, by lightning meetings and political demonstrations against tsardom.

These new tactics were vehemently combated by the opportunist majority of the Messameh Dassy, who had strong leanings towards "Economism," shunned revolutionary methods, and were opposed to the political struggle against the autocracy being waged "on the streets." Led by Stalin, the revolutionary minority of the Messameh Dassy put up a fierce and implacable fight against the opportunists on behalf of the new tactics, the tactics of mass political agitation. In this they had the hearty support of the advanced workers of Tiflis.

* L. Beria, *On the History of the Bolshevik Organizations in Transcaucasia*, Moscow 1949, pp. 28, 29.

A prominent part in inducing the Social-Democrats of Tiflis to adopt the new methods was played by Victor Kurnatovsky, an accomplished Marxist and a staunch supporter and close colleague of Lenin's, who did much to spread the latter's ideas in Transcaucasia. He came to Tiflis in the autumn of 1900, and there formed close contact with Stalin and the revolutionary minority of the Messameh Dassy, and became an intimate friend and comrade of Stalin's.

When Lenin's *Iskra* began to appear in December 1900, Stalin completely identified himself with its policy. It was at once clear to him that Lenin was the creator of a real Marxist Party, a leader and a teacher.

"My knowledge of Lenin's revolutionary activities since the end of the 'nineties, and especially after 1901, after the appearance of *Iskra*," Stalin says, "had convinced me that in Lenin we had a man of extraordinary calibre. I did not regard him as a mere leader of the Party, but as its actual founder, for he alone understood the inner essence and urgent needs of our Party. When I compared him with the other leaders of our Party, it always seemed to me that he was head and shoulders above his colleagues—Plekhanov, Martov, Axelrod and the others; that, compared with them, Lenin was not just one of the leaders, but a leader of the highest rank, a mountain eagle, who knew no fear in the struggle, and who boldly led the Party forward along the unexplored paths of the Russian revolutionary movement."*

Stalin conceived a boundless faith in Lenin's revolutionary genius. He took Lenin's path as his own. From this path he has never swerved; and when Lenin died, he confidently and courageously carried on his work.

In 1900 and 1901, when an economic crisis had set in, under the influence of the working-class movement in Russia and as a result of the activities of the revolutionary Social-Democrats, a series of economic strikes broke out in Tiflis, spreading from factory to factory. August 1900 witnessed a huge strike at the railway shops and locomotive yards, an active part in which was played by Mikhail Kalinin, who had been exiled to the Caucasus from St. Petersburg. On April 22, 1901, a May Day demonstration was held in the centre of Tiflis, organized and led by Stalin. This demonstration was hailed by Lenin's *Iskra* as an event of historic importance for the whole of the Caucasus; it was to exercise an enormous influence on the entire subsequent course of the working-class movement in the Caucasus.

Thus, guided by the revolutionary minority of the Messameh Dassy headed by Stalin, the working-class movement of Georgia passed in those years from propaganda activities confined to narrow cir-

* J. V. Stalin, *Collected Works*, Russ. ed., Vol. 6, pp. 52-53.

J.V. STALIN
Photo 1900

cles to political agitation among the masses; and in the Caucasus too there began to be carried out that uniting of Socialism with the working-class movement which had been so brilliantly effected several years earlier by the St. Petersburg League of Struggle, under Lenin's leadership.

The tsarist government was alarmed by the growing revolutionary struggle of the Transcaucasian proletariat and resorted to sterner measures of repression than ever, hoping in this way to halt the movement. On March 21, 1901, the police made a search of the physical observatory where Stalin worked and had his quarters. This search, and the warrant which he learned had been issued by the secret police for his arrest, induced Stalin to go into hiding. From that moment and right up to the revolution of February 1917 he lived the underground life, full of heroism and unflagging effort, of a professional revolutionary of the Lenin school.

The tsarist satraps were powerless to halt the growth of the revolutionary movement. In September 1901, *Brdzola* (*Struggle*), the first illegal Social-Democratic newspaper in Georgia, started publication. Founded on the initiative of Stalin and Ketskhoveli, it consistently advocated the principles of Lenin's *Iskra*. As a Marxist newspaper in Russia, *Brdzola* was second only to *Iskra*.

The editorial in its first issue (September 1901) was written by Stalin. Entitled "From the Editors," it defined the aims and objects of the newspaper. Stalin wrote: "The Georgian Social-Democratic newspaper must provide plain answers to all questions connected with the labour movement, explain questions of principle, explain theoretically the role the working class plays in the struggle, and throw the light of scientific Socialism upon every phenomenon the workers encounter."*

The paper, Stalin said in the editorial, must lead the labour movement, it must keep in the closest possible contact with the working masses, be in a position to influence them constantly, and act as their intellectual and guiding centre.

The next issue of *Brdzola* (November-December 1901) contained an important article by Stalin, "The Russian Social-Democratic Party and Its Immediate Tasks." In it Stalin stressed the necessity of uniting scientific Socialism with the spontaneous working-class movement and the role of the working class as the leader of the democratic emancipation movement; he demonstrated the need for the foundation of an independent political party of the proletariat.

Leaflets in the various languages of multinational Transcaucasia were also published on a wide scale. "Every district in Tiflis has been inundated with splendidly written leaflets in Russian, Georgian and Armenian," wrote Lenin's *Iskra,* in reference to the

---

* J. V. Stalin, *Collected Works*, Russ. ed., Vol. 1, p. 9.

activities of the Tiflis Social-Democrats.* Lado Kets-khoveli, Stalin's closest colleague, organized a Committee of the Leninist *Iskra* trend in Baku and set up a secret printing plant there. On November 11, 1901, at a conference of the Tiflis Social-Democratic organization, a Tiflis Committee of the R.S.D.L.P. was elected, one of whose members was Stalin. But Stalin did not stay in Tiflis long. At the end of November, on the instructions of the Tiflis Committee, he went to Batum, the third largest proletarian centre in the Caucasus (Baku was the first and Tiflis the second), to form a Social-Democratic organization there.

In Batum, Stalin launched vigorously into revolutionary work: he established contact with politically-advanced workers, formed Social-Democratic study circles, some of which he conducted himself, set up a secret printing plant, wrote, printed and distributed stirring leaflets, directed the struggle of the workers at the Rothschild and Mantashev plants, and organized revolutionary propaganda in the countryside. He formed a Social-Democratic Party organization in Batum and a Batum Committee of the R.S.D.L.P., and led industrial strikes. He organized and directed the famous political demonstration of the Batum workers on March 9, 1902, himself marching at the head of the columns. This was a practi-

* *Iskra,* No. 25, September 15, 1902.

cal example of the combination of strikes with political demonstrations.

Thus, in this period, in a determined and implacable struggle against opportunism, a Leninist *Iskra*ist organization grew up in Transcaucasia. Its most prominent organizer and leader was Stalin, who was already known among the Batum workers as the "workers' teacher." This organization was founded on the sound principles of proletarian internationalism, uniting, as it did, politically advanced proletarians of different nationalities—Georgians, Armenians, Azerbaijanians and Russians. In later days, Lenin time and again cited the Transcaucasian Party organization as a model of proletarian internationalism.

The rising militancy of the Batum workers was a cause of serious uneasiness to the government. Police sleuths scoured the city, looking for the "ringleaders." On April 5, 1902, Stalin was arrested. But even while in prison (first in Batum, then in Kutais—a jail notorious for the severity of its regime, to which he was transferred on April 19, 1903—and then back again in Batum), Stalin never severed his contacts with the revolutionary work.

In the early part of March 1903 the Caucasian Social-Democratic organizations held their first congress, at which a Caucasian Union of the R.S.D.L.P. was set up. Although in confinement, Stalin was elected to the Committee of the Caucasian Union. It was while in prison that Stalin learned from delegates

returned from the Second Party Co[…]
profound dissensions between the Bols[…]
Mensheviks. Stalin determinedly took[…]
the side of Lenin, of the Bolsheviks.

In the autumn of 1903, Stalin was banished for
three years to Novaya Uda, a village in the Bala-
gansk District, Province of Irkutsk, Eastern Siberia.
He arrived there on November 27, 1903. While in
exile he received a letter from Lenin.

"I first became acquainted with Lenin in 1903,"
Stalin subsequently related. "True, it was not a personal acquaintance; it was maintained by correspondence. But it made an indelible impression upon me,
one which has never left me throughout all my work
in the Party. I was in exile in Siberia at the time....
Lenin's note was comparatively short, but it contained a bold and fearless criticism of the practical
work of our Party, and a remarkably clear and con-
cise account of the entire plan of work of the Party
in the immediate future."*

Stalin did not stay in exile long. He was impa-
tient to be back at liberty, to set to work to carry
out Lenin's plan for the building of a Bolshevik
Party. On January 5, 1904, he escaped from exile,
and in February 1904 he was back again in the
Caucasus, first in Batum, and then in Tiflis.

---

* J. V. Stalin, *Collected Works*, Russ. ed., Vol. 6
pp. 52, 53.

★

III

S TALIN HAD SPENT almost two years in prison and exile. During this period the tide of revolution had been steadily rising in the country. The Second Congress of the R.S.D.L.P. had taken place, at which the victory of Marxism over "Economism" had been consolidated. But those old opportunists, the "Economists," smashed by the Party, were superseded by a new type of opportunists, the Mensheviks. After the Congress Lenin and the Bolsheviks launched a fierce struggle against the Mensheviks, against their opportunist ideas and their attempts to split and disorganize the Party. With the outbreak of the Russo-Japanese War and the gathering revolutionary storm, this struggle took on an even more acute form. Lenin considered that only a new Party congress (the third) could offer a way out of the crisis in the Party. To secure the convocation of this congress was now the principal task of all the Bolsheviks.

In the Caucasus, Lenin's faithful mainstay in this campaign was Stalin, the leader of the Transcaucasian Bolsheviks. During this period he concentrated his energies on the fierce fight against Menshevism. A member of the Committee of the Caucasian Union of the R.S.D.L.P., he, together with Tskhakaya, directed the committee's activities. He was indefatigable: he periodically toured Transcaucasia, visiting Batum, Chiaturi, Kutais, Tiflis, Baku and the rural districts of Western Georgia, strengthening the old Party organizations and forming new ones, taking part in the fierce controversies with the Mensheviks and other enemies of Marxism at numerous discussions, stoutly upholding the Bolshevik views and exposing the political chicanery and opportunism of the Mensheviks and of those who were prone to compromise with them.

Under the leadership of Stalin and Djaparidze, "in December 1904 a huge strike of the Baku workers took place; it lasted from December 13 to December 31 and ended with the conclusion of a collective agreement with the oil magnates, the first collective agreement in the history of the working-class movement in Russia.

"The Baku strike marked the beginning of the revolutionary upsurge in Transcaucasia.

"The Baku strike served as the 'signal for the glorious actions in January and February all over Russia' (*Stalin*)."*

"This strike," says the *History of the C.P.S.U.(B.)* "was like a clap of thunder heralding a great revolutionary storm" in Russia.

---

* L. Beria, *On the History of the Bolshevik Organizations in Transcaucasia*, Moscow 1949, p. 79.

Stalin persistently worked in accordance with Lenin's directives. He advocated and developed the Bolshevik ideas before the masses, and organized the struggle for the convocation of a Third Party Congress. Close contact was maintained between Lenin and the Committee of the Caucasian Union all through this period. It was Stalin who led the ideological and political fight of the Caucasian Bolsheviks against the Mensheviks, Socialist-Revolutionaries, nationalists and anarchists in the period of the first Russian Revolution. A most effective weapon of the Bolsheviks in this fight was their party literature; and practically every Bolshevik publication that came out in the Caucasus owed its origin to Stalin's initiative and efforts, thanks to which the production of illegal books, newspapers, pamphlets and leaflets attained dimensions unprecedented in tsarist Russia.

One remarkably bold enterprise of the Caucasian Union Committee of the R.S.D.L.P., and an outstanding example of the Bolshevik technique of underground work, was the Avlabar secret printing press, which functioned in Tiflis from November 1903 to April 1906. On this press were printed Lenin's *The Revolutionary-Democratic Dictatorship of the Proletariat and the Peasantry* and *To the Rural Poor,* Stalin's *Briefly About the Disagreements in the Party, Two Clashes* and other pamphlets, the Party program and rules, and scores of leaflets, many of which were written by Stalin. On it, too, were printed the newspapers *Proletariatis Brdzola* (*The Proletarian Struggle*) and *Proletariatis Brdzolis Purtseli* (*Herald of the Proletarian Struggle*). Books, pamphlets, newspapers and leaflets were published in Russian, Georgian and Armenian and were printed in several thousands of copies.

A decisive role in the defence of the principles of Bolshevism in the Caucasus and in the propagation and development of Lenin's ideas was played by the newspaper *Proletariatis Brdzola,* edited by Stalin, the organ of the Caucasian Union of the R.S.D.L.P. and a worthy successor of *Brdzola.* For its size and its quality as a Bolshevik newspaper, *Proletariatis Brdzola* was second only to *Proletary,* the Central Organ of the Party, edited by Lenin. Practically every issue carried articles by Lenin, reprinted from the *Proletary.* Many highly important articles were written by Stalin. In them he stands forth as a talented controversialist, eminent Party writer and theoretician, political leader of the proletariat, and faithful follower of Lenin. In his articles and pamphlets, Stalin worked out a number of theoretical and political problems. He disclosed the ideological fallacies of the anti-Bolshevik trends and factions, their opportunism and treachery. Every blow at the enemy struck with telling effect. Lenin paid glowing tribute to *Proletariatis Brdzola,* to its Marxian consistency and high literary merit.

Lenin's most loyal disciple and associate and the most consistent champion of his ideas, Stalin played an outstanding part in the ideological discomfiture of Menshevism in the Caucasus, and in the defence of the fundamental ideological, organizational and tactical principles of the Marxist party. His writings of that period are a model of consistency in the advocacy of Lenin's views, and are distinguished for their theoretical penetration and uncompromising hostility to opportunism.

His remarkable pamphlet *Briefly About the Disagreements in the Party*, his two "Letters From Kutais" and his article "Reply to 'Social-Democrat'" are a vigorous defence of the ideological fundamentals of the Marxist party.

The "Letters From Kutais" (September-October 1904) contain a trenchant criticism of Plekhanov's articles in the new, Menshevik *Iskra* taking issue with Lenin's *What Is To Be Done?* Comrade Stalin consistently defends Lenin's views on the question of spontaneity and consciousness in the labour movement. He writes:

"The conclusion (practical deduction) to be drawn from this is as follows: we must raise the proletariat to a consciousness of its true class interests, to a consciousness of the Socialist ideal, and not break this ideal up into small change, or adjust it to the spontaneous movement. Lenin has laid down the theoretical basis on which this practical deduction is built. It is enough to accept this theoretical premise and no opportunism will get anywhere near you. Herein lies the significance of Lenin's idea. I call it Lenin's, because nobody in Russian literature has expressed it with such clarity as Lenin."*

Briefly About the Disagreements in the Party (written at the beginning of 1905 and published illegally in May of that year) was an outstanding contribution to Bolshevik thought. It had a direct kinship with Lenin's historic work *What Is To Be Done?*, and resolutely upheld and developed the ideas of that genius.

Developing Lenin's ideas, Comrade Stalin in this pamphlet argues the supreme importance of Socialist consciousness to the labour movement. At the same time he warns against one-sidedly exaggerating the importance of ideas and forgetting the conditions of economic development and the role of the labour movement. Can it be said, Stalin asks, that Socialism is everything and the labour movement nothing? "Of course not! Only idealists say that. Some day, in a very long time to come, economic development will inevitably bring the working class to the social revolution, and, consequently, compel it to break off all connection with bourgeois ideology. The only point is that this path is a very long and painful one."**

* J. V. Stalin, *Collected Works*, Russ. ed., Vol. 1, p. 58.
** *Ibid.*, p. 105.

After profoundly arguing the question of the relation between the spontaneous labour movement and Socialist consciousness from all aspects and angles, Comrade Stalin in the pamphlet, *Briefly About the Disagreements in the Party,* sums up the views of the Lenin wing of Social-Democracy on this subject as follows:

"What is scientific Socialism *without the labour movement?*—A compass which, if left unused, can only grow rusty and then has to be thrown overboard.

"What is the labour movement *without Socialism?*—A ship without a compass which will reach the other shore in any case, but would reach it much sooner and with less danger if it had a compass.

"Unite the two and you will get a splendid vessel, which will speed straight towards the other shore and reach its haven unharmed.

"Unite the labour movement with Socialism and you will get a Social-Democratic movement which will speed straight towards the 'promised land.' "*

The whole history of the working-class struggle in Russia has brilliantly confirmed this important theoretical conclusion of Comrade Stalin's. In the pamphlet in question Stalin subjected the opportunist theory of spontaneity to withering criticism and gave a reasoned explanation of the role and significance

* J. V. Stalin, *Collected Works*, Russ. ed., Vol. 1, pp. 102-03.

of a revolutionary party and of revolutionary theory for the working class.

"The labour movement," wrote Stalin, "must be united with Socialism; practical activities and theoretical thought must merge into one and thereby lend the spontaneous labour movement a Social-Democratic character.... Our duty, the duty of Social-Democracy is to deflect the spontaneous labour movement from the path of narrow trade-unionism to the Social-Democratic path. Our duty is to introduce Socialist consciousness[1] into this movement and unite the advanced forces of the working class in one centralized party. Our task is always to be at the head of the movement and tirelessly combat all those—foes or 'friends'—who hinder the accomplishment of this task."*

Stalin's writings met with Lenin's wholehearted approval. Reviewing in the *Proletary* (No. 22), the Central Organ of the Party, Stalin's "Reply to 'Social-Democrat'," which appeared in the *Proletariatis Brdzola* in August 1905, Lenin noted the "excellent formulation of the famous question of the 'introduction of consciousness from without.'"

Stalin wrote a number of articles in support of Lenin's line at and after the Second Congress of the R.S.D.L.P. In an article entitled "The Proletarian

---

[1] which *was worked out* by Marx and Engels.
* *Ibid.*, pp. 105, 106.

Class and the Proletarian Party" (*Proletariatis Brdzola*, No. 8, January 1, 1905), dealing with the first paragraph of the Party Rules, he upheld the organizational principles of the Party, fully holding by Lenin's teachings regarding the Party, and developing and substantiating Lenin's ideas. This article was a defence of the Bolshevik principles of organization as propounded by Lenin in his famous book *One Step Forward, Two Steps Back*.

"Up till now," Stalin wrote, "our Party has resembled a hospitable patriarchal family, ready to take in all who sympathize. But now that our Party has become a centralized *organization*, it has thrown off its patriarchal aspect and has become in all respects like a *fortress*, the gates of which are opened only to those who are worthy. And this is of great importance to us. At a time when the autocracy is trying to corrupt the class consciousness of the proletariat with 'trade-unionism,' nationalism, clericalism and the like, and when, on the other hand, the liberal intelligentsia is persistently striving to kill the political independence of the proletariat and to impose its tutelage upon it—at such a time we must be extremely vigilant and never forget that our Party is a *fortress*, the gates of which are opened only to those who have been tested."*

---

* J. V. Stalin, *Collected Works*, Russ. ed., Vol. 1, p. 67.

The article "The Social-Democratic View of the National Question" (*Proletariatis Brdzola,* No. 7, September 1, 1904) is a brilliant commentary on the national program of the R.S.D.L.P. In it Stalin substantiates and explains the theory and program of the Party on the national question, subjects the opportunist principle of dividing the proletariat into national sections to devastating criticism, and consistently advocates the internationalist type of proletarian class organization. Stalin here reveals himself as an outstanding theoretician of the national question, with a perfect mastery of the Marxist dialectical method. He foreshadows the ideas which he subsequently developed in his *Marxism and the National Question.*

In the first Russian Revolution Stalin from the very outset resolutely advocated and practised Lenin's strategy and tactics of the revolution, his idea of the *hegemony of the proletariat* in the revolution.

Of the Liberals, who were out, not for revolution, but for reconciliation with the tsar, Stalin had written on the eve of January 9, 1905: "Yes, gentlemen, vain are your efforts! The Russian Revolution is inevitable. It is as inevitable as the rising of the sun! Can you prevent the sun from rising? *The main force in this revolution is the urban and rural proletariat, its banner-bearer is the Social-Democratic Labour Party,* and not you, Messieurs Liberals!"*

---

* *Ibid.,* p. 78.

With equal vigour, Stalin supported Lenin's idea of armed insurrection as the means of overthrowing the autocracy and establishing a republic. The necessity for armed insurrection is exhaustively demonstrated in his writings of 1905-07. "The salvation of the people lies in a victorious uprising of the people themselves," he says. Like Lenin, he attached immense importance to proper technical preparation for insurrection, the formation of fighting squads, the procurement of arms, and so forth. "It is the *technical guidance and organizational preparation of the all-Russian insurrection* that constitute the new tasks with which life has confronted the proletariat," he wrote.* Stalin himself gave day-to-day guidance to the Bolshevik organizations in Transcaucasia in preparing for armed insurrection.

Stalin explained and developed Lenin's idea of a provisional revolutionary government. The formation of such a government, he argued, should be the natural outcome of a victorious armed insurrection of the people. Since it is the proletariat and the peasantry that will triumph in the insurrection, the provisional revolutionary government must be the spokesman of their aspirations and interests. Such a government must be a revolutionary dictatorship of the proletariat and the peasantry. Only the dictatorship of these revolutionary classes will be able to

* J. V. Stalin, *Collected Works*, Russ. ed., Vol. 1, p. 133

curb and suppress the sinister forces of reaction, arm the people, carry out the minimum program of the R.S.D.L.P., and consolidate and consummate the victory of the revolution.

"If the advanced proletariat is the leader of the revolution," Stalin wrote, "and if it must take an active part in organizing the insurrection—then it is self-evident that we cannot wash our hands of and remain aloof from the provisional revolutionary government, that we must conquer political power in conjunction with the peasantry and take part in the provisional government[1]: the leader of the revolutionary street must also be the leader of the revolution's government."*

In the fight against the numerous foes of the Bolshevik Party and the working class, Stalin consistently advocated and elaborated Lenin's theory of the revolution and his tactical plan. It was the supreme merit of this plan that it was adapted in a most remarkable degree to the realities of the situation in Russia, that it rallied broad masses of the people to the fight and inspired them with confidence in victory, that it advanced the revolution.

The Caucasian Union Committee indefatigably propagated the decisions of the Third Party Congress and summoned the workers and peasants to

---

[1] Here we are not dealing with the principles underlying the question.

* *Ibid*, pp. 258-59.

armed insurrection. Stalin's leaflets of the year 1905 are a model of the propaganda of Bolshevik ideas among the masses. In his "Armed Insurrection and Our Tactics," "The Provisional Revolutionary Government and Social-Democracy," "Reaction Is Growing" and other articles, he castigated the Menshevik leaders and insistently advocated and preached the necessity for armed insurrection.

The general strike of October 1905 demonstrated the strength, the might of the proletarian movement and impelled the mortally terrified tsar to issue his Manifesto of October 17. Unstinting in its promises of all sorts of liberties to the people, this Manifesto was nothing but a fraud on the masses, a stratagem designed to secure a breathing space, which the tsar needed in order to fool the gullible, gain time and marshal his forces for a blow at the revolution. The Bolsheviks warned the masses that the Manifesto was a trap. The October Manifesto found Stalin in Tiflis, in the heat of the fight for Lenin's tactical plan, for the Bolshevik slogans in the revolution. Addressing a meeting of workers on October 18, Stalin said:

"What do we need in order to really win? We need three things: first—arms, second—arms, third—arms and arms again!"*

---

* *History of the C.P.S.U.(B.), Short Course,* Moscow 1949, p. 99.

Insisting that the victory of the revolution demanded a nation-wide armed insurrection, Stalin, in a leaflet headed "Citizens!" issued by the Tiflis Committee of the Caucasian Union of the R.S.D.L.P., which he wrote in October 1905, said:

"The general political strike now raging—which is of dimensions unprecedented and unexampled not only in the history of Russia but in the history of the whole world—may, perhaps, end today without developing into a nation-wide uprising, but tomorrow it will shake the country again with even greater force and develop into that grand armed uprising which must settle the age-long contest between the Russian people and the tsarist autocracy and smash the head of this despicable monster.... A nation-wide armed uprising—such is the supreme task that today confronts the proletariat of Russia, and is imperatively demanding execution!"*

Stalin's revolutionary activities in Transcaucasia at this period were immense. Under his guidance the Fourth Bolshevik Conference of the Caucasian Union of the R.S.D.L.P. (November 1905) passed a decision to intensify the struggle for preparing and carrying out armed insurrection, for boycotting the tsarist Duma and for extending and consolidating the revolutionary organizations of the workers and peasants—the Soviets of Workers' Deputies, the strike commit-

---

* J. V. Stalin, *Collected Works*, Russ. ed., Vol. 1, p. 186.

tees and the revolutionary peasant committees. Stalin exposed and denounced the Mensheviks as opponents of the revolution and of armed insurrection. He worked assiduously to prepare the workers for the decisive battle with the autocracy. The flames of revolution swept all over Transcaucasia. Special mention of the activities of the Bolshevik organizations in Transcaucasia was made at the Third Congress of the Party, in the resolution on "The Events in the Caucasus," moved by Lenin, which referred to these organizations as "the most militant in our Party" and called upon the whole Party to lend them the utmost support.

In December 1905, Stalin went to Tammerfors (Finland) to attend the first All-Russian Bolshevik Conference as a delegate from the Transcaucasian Bolsheviks. It was here that Lenin and Stalin first met. Stalin worked with Lenin on the political (drafting) committee of the Conference, to which he was elected, as one of the prominent leaders of the Party.

With the defeat of the December armed uprising, the tide of revolution gradually began to ebb. The conflict between the Bolsheviks and Mensheviks flared up afresh with the preparations for the Fourth Congress of the R.S.D.L.P. Anarcho-syndicalist elements came on to the scene, and were particularly obstreperous in Tiflis. Stalin continued to lead the struggle against all anti-proletarian trends in Transcaucasia.

Stalin took an active part in the Fourth Congress of the R.S.D.L.P. (Stockholm, April 1906), where, together with Lenin, he upheld the Bolshevik line in the revolution against the Mensheviks. Replying to the Mensheviks, Stalin put the question squarely:

"Either the hegemony of the proletariat, or the hegemony of the democratic bourgeoisie—that is how the question stands in the Party, that is where we differ."*

Shortly after the Congress, Stalin wrote a pamphlet entitled *The Present Situation and the Unity Congress of the Workers' Party*, in which he analyzed the lessons of the December armed uprising, vindicated the Bolshevik line in the revolution and summed up the results of the Fourth Congress of the R.S.D.L.P.

After the Congress Stalin returned to Transcaucasia, where he continued his uncompromising fight against Menshevism and other anti-proletarian trends. He directed the *Akhali Tskhovreba* (*New Life*), *Akhali Droyeba* (*New Times*), *Chveni Tskhovreba* (*Our Life*) and *Dro* (*Time*), Bolshevik newspapers published legally in the Georgian language in Tiflis.

It was at this period that Stalin wrote the remarkable series of articles under the title "Anarchism or Socialism?" in connection with the increased

---

* J. V. Stalin, *Collected Works*, Russ. ed., Vol. 1, p. 240.

activities of anarchists of the Kropotkin school in Transcaucasia.

With the ebb of the revolution and the reaction that followed in its wake, the Party was called upon, as a direct Party task, to defend the theoretical foundations of Bolshevism. In 1909 Lenin published his work of genius, *Materialism and Empirio-Criticism,* in which he thoroughly exposed the backsliders from Marxian theory and vindicated the theoretical foundations of the Bolshevik Party.

Stalin, too, rose up in defence of the theoretical foundations of Marxism. In his articles "Anarchism or Socialism?" he upheld and developed the theoretical tenets of the Marxist party—dialectical and historical materialism. They were published in 1906 and 1907 in Georgian Bolshevik newspapers. They explained the meaning of materialism and dialectics and the principles of historical materialism in simple and popular style, at the same time formulating and answering with supreme penetration the fundamental questions of Marxist-Leninist theory: the inevitability and inavertibility of the Socialist revolution and the dictatorship of the proletariat, and the necessity for a militant proletarian party, a party of a *new* type, differing from the old, reformist parties of the Second International. They also expounded the basic principles of the strategy and tactics of the Party. These articles are an important contribution to the theory of Marxism-Leninism and form part of the ideological treasury of our Party. In their profound treatment of the theory of Marxism-Leninism in inseparable connection with the urgent tasks of the revolutionary class struggle of the proletariat, they are exemplary.

Stalin took an active part in the work of the Fifth Congress of the R.S.D.L.P., held in London in April and May 1907, at which the victory of the Bolsheviks over the Mensheviks was sealed. On his return, he published an article, "The London Congress of the Russian Social-Democratic Labour Party (Notes of a Delegate)," in which he examined the decisions and results of the Congress, defended the ideological and tactical position of the Bolsheviks, denounced the bourgeois-liberal line of the Mensheviks in the revolution and their policy of liquidating the Party, and revealed the class nature of Menshevism, showing that it was a petty-bourgeois political trend.

★

THE FIRST Russian Revolution ended in defeat. Between the first and the second revolutions there intervened a period of ten years, during which the Bolsheviks worked perseveringly and indefatigably, with heroism and self-sacrifice to organize the masses, to foster in them the revolutionary spirit, to guide their struggles and to prepare the ground for the future victory of the revolution.

For Lenin and Stalin these were years of relentless struggle for the preservation and consolidation of the underground revolutionary Party, for the application of the Bolshevik line in the new conditions; they were years of strenuous effort to organize and educate the masses of the working class, and of unusually stubborn struggle against tsarism. The tsarist authorities sensed in Stalin a revolutionary of formidable calibre, and were at great pains to deprive him of all opportunity of carrying on revolutionary work. Arrest, imprisonment and exile followed each other in succession. Between 1902 and 1913, Stalin was arrested seven times and exiled six times. Five times he escaped from exile. Scarcely had the tsarist myrmidons convoyed him to a new place of exile than he would again be "at large," to resume his work of mustering the revolutionary energies of the masses. His last exile, in Turukhansk, was the only one that was not cut short in this way; from that he was freed by the revolution of February 1917.

In June 1907 began the Baku period of Stalin's revolutionary activity. On his return from the Fifth (London) Congress of the R.S.D.L.P., he left Tiflis and on the instructions of the Party settled in Baku, the largest industrial area in Transcaucasia and one of the most important centres of the working-class movement in Russia. Here he threw himself into the work of rallying the Baku organization around Lenin's slogans and of lining up the working masses under the banner of Bolshevism. He organized the fight to oust the Mensheviks from the working-class districts of Baku (Balakhani, Bibi-Eibat, Chorny Gorod and Byely Gorod). He directed the Bolshevik illegal and legal publications (*Bakinsky Proletary, Gudok* and *Bakinsky Rabochy*). He directed the campaign in the elections of the workers' deputies to the Third Duma. The "Mandate to the Social-Democratic Deputies of the Third State Duma," written by Stalin, was adopted at a meeting of representatives of the workers' curia in Baku on September 22, 1907. Stalin guided the struggle of the Baku workers. The big campaign he led in connection with the negotiations for a collective agreement between the oil workers and employers was a brilliant application of Lenin's policy of flexibly combining illegal and legal activities in the period of reaction. He secured the victory of the Bolsheviks in this campaign by skilfully applying Lenin's tactics of rallying the workers for a political struggle against the tsarist monarchy. Amid the gloomy night of the Stolypin reaction, proletarian Baku presented an unusual spectacle, with the proletarian struggle seething, and the voice of Stalin's creations, the legal Bolshevik newspapers, reverberating throughout Russia. "The last of the Mohicans of the mass political strike!"* was Lenin's comment on the heroic struggle of the Baku workers in 1908.

Stalin rallied around him a sturdy body of tried Bolshevik-Leninists—Fioletov, Saratovets (Efimov), Vatsek, Bokov, Malygin, Orjonikidze, Djaparidze, Shaumyan, Spandaryan, Khanlar, Memedov, Azizbekov, Kiazi-Mamed and others—and finally he secured the complete triumph of Bolshevism in the Baku Party organization. Baku became a citadel of Bolshevism. Under Stalin's leadership, the Baku proletariat waged a heroic struggle in the front ranks of the Russian revolutionary movement.

The Baku period was of major importance in Stalin's life and work. This is what he himself says of it:

* V. I. Lenin, *Collected Works*, 3rd Russ. ed., Vol. XV, p. 33.

"Three years of revolutionary activity among the workers in the oil industry steeled me as a practical fighter and as one of the practical local leaders. Contact with advanced workers in Baku, with men like Vatsek, Saratovets and Fioletov, on the one hand, and the storm of acute conflicts between the workers and oil owners, on the other, first taught me what leading large masses of workers meant. It was in Baku that I thus received my second revolutionary baptism of fire."*

On March 25, 1908, Stalin was arrested and, after spending nearly eight months in prison, was exiled to Solvychegodsk, in the Province of Vologda, for a term of two years. But on June 24, 1909, he escaped from exile and made his way back to Baku, to continue his illegal work. He vigorously and unreservedly supported Lenin in his stand against the Liquidators and Otzovists. His historic "Letters From the Caucasus" appeared in the central Party press, and for the newspaper *Bakinsky Proletary* he wrote "The Party Crisis and Our Tasks," "From the Party" and other articles in which he boldly criticized the state of the Party organizations and outlined a plan to put an end to the crisis in the Party. In these writings Stalin subjected the Liquidators to devastating criticism, using the example of the Tiflis Mensheviks to illustrate the renegacy of the Liquidators on

---

* J. V. Stalin, *Collected Works*, Russ. ed., Vol. 8, p. 174.

questions of program and tactics. He severely condemned the treacherous conduct of the accomplices of Trotskyism, and formulated the immediate tasks of the Party, to which the Prague Party Conference subsequently gave effect, namely, the convocation of a general Party conference, the publication of a legal Party newspaper and the establishment of an illegal Party centre to conduct the practical work in Russia.

On March 23, 1910, Stalin was again arrested in Baku, and, after spending six months in prison, was again exiled to Solvychegodsk. While in exile he established contact with Lenin, and towards the end of 1910, wrote a letter to the Central Committee in which he expressed full solidarity with Lenin's tactics of forming a Party bloc of all who favoured the preservation and consolidation of the illegal proletarian party. In this letter he castigated the "rank unprincipledness" of Trotsky and outlined a plan for the organization of Party work in Russia.

In the latter half of 1911 began the St. Petersburg period of Comrade Stalin's revolutionary activities. On September 6 he secretly left Vologda for St. Petersburg. He established contact with the Party organization there, and directed its attention to the need to fight against the Liquidators—Mensheviks and Trotskyites—and to rally and strengthen the St. Petersburg Bolshevik organizations. He was arrested in St. Petersburg on September 9, 1911, and sent back to the Vologda Province, whence he again managed to escape in February 1912.

In January 1912, a momentous event took place in the life of the Party. The Prague Conference of the R.S.D.L.P., having expelled the Mensheviks, inaugurated a party of a new type—the Party of Leninism, the Bolshevik Party.

For this new type of party the Bolsheviks had been working ever since the days of the old *Iskra*—working persistently and perseveringly, regardless of all obstacles. The whole history of the fight against the "Economists," the Mensheviks, the Trotskyites, the Otzovists, the idealists of all shades, down to the empirio-criticists, had been paving the way for the formation of such a party. Of prime and decisive importance in this preparatory work were Lenin's *What Is To Be Done?, One Step Forward, Two Steps Back, Two Tactics of Social-Democracy in the Democratic Revolution,* and *Materialism and Empirio-Criticism. Stalin was Lenin's faithful associate in this struggle against innumerable enemies, his loyal support in the fight for a revolutionary Marxist party, a Bolshevik Party.*

★

IV

THE PRAGUE Conference predicted a revolutionary revival in the near future and made every provision to enable the Party to meet it fully prepared. It elected a Bolshevik Central Committee, set up a centre to direct the practical revolutionary work in Russia (the Russian Bureau of the Central Committee), and decided to publish the *Pravda* newspaper. Stalin, who had been an agent of the Central Committee since 1910, was elected to the Central Committee in his absence. On Lenin's proposal, he was put in charge of the Russian Bureau of the Central Committee. But Stalin was in exile, and arrangements for his flight had to be made. On Lenin's instructions, Sergo Orjonikidze went to Vologda to inform Stalin of the decisions of the Prague Conference. Then, on February 29, 1912, Stalin again escaped from exile. He had a brief spell of liberty, which he turned to good account: on the instructions of the Central Committee, he toured the most important districts of Russia, made preparations for the coming May Day demonstration, wrote the well-known May Day leaflet of the Central Committee, and edited the Bolshevik weekly *Zvezda* in St. Petersburg during the strikes that followed the shooting down of the workers in the Lena gold fields.

A powerful instrument used by the Bolshevik Party to strengthen its organizations and to spread its influence among the masses was the Bolshevik daily newspaper *Pravda,* published in St. Petersburg. It was founded according to Lenin's instructions, on the initiative of Stalin. It was under Stalin's direction that the first issue was prepared and the policy of the paper decided.

Pravda was founded simultaneously with the new rise of the revolutionary movement. Its first issue appeared on April 22 (May 5, New Style), 1912. This was a day of real celebration for the workers. It is in honour of *Pravda*'s appearance that it was later decided to celebrate May 5 as Workers' Press Day.

"The *Pravda* of 1912," Comrade Stalin wrote on the occasion of the tenth anniversary of the paper, "was the laying of the cornerstone of the victory of Bolshevism in 1917."*

On April 22, 1912, Stalin was arrested on the streets of St. Petersburg. After several months in prison, he was exiled again, for a term of three years, this time to a more remote region—Narym. But on September 1, 1912, he once more escaped and returned to St. Petersburg. Here he edited the Bolshevik

---

* J. V. Stalin, *Collected Works*, Russ. ed., Vol. 5, p. 128.

Pravda and directed the Bolshevik campaign in the elections to the Fourth Duma. At great risk, for the police were constantly on his track, he addressed a number of meetings at factories. But the workers themselves and their organizations kept close guard on Stalin and protected him from the police.

A most important part in the election campaign, which culminated in a victory for the Party, was played by the "Mandate of the Workingmen of St. Petersburg to Their Labour Deputy," written by Stalin. Lenin gave a very high appraisal of the Mandate; when sending the copy to the press, he wrote on the margin: "*Return* without fail!! Keep clean. *Highly important* to preserve this document!" In a letter to the editors of *Pravda*, he wrote: "Publish this Mandate to the St. Petersburg Deputy without fail, in a prominent place in large type."* Stalin's Mandate reminded the workers of the unaccomplished tasks of the 1905 Revolution and summoned them to a revolutionary struggle, a struggle on two fronts— against the tsarist government and against the liberal bourgeoisie, which was seeking to come to terms with tsardom. After the elections Stalin guided the activities of the Bolshevik section of the Social-Democratic group in the Duma. With Stalin in St. Petersburg worked Y. Sverdlov and V. Molotov, who

* V. I. Lenin, *Collected Works*, 3rd Russ. ed., Vol. XXIX, p. 78.

took an active part in editing the *Pravda,* in the election campaign and in guiding the Bolshevik group in the Duma. At this period contact between Lenin and Stalin became still closer. In his letters Lenin expressed his entire approval of Stalin's activities and of his speeches and articles. On two occasions Stalin went to Cracow, where Lenin was then residing: once in November 1912, and again at the end of December 1912, to attend conferences of the Central Committee with Party workers.

It was while he was abroad that Stalin wrote *Marxism and the National Question,* on which Lenin set the highest value. "The principles of the Social-Democratic national program," Lenin wrote, "have already been dealt with recently in Marxian literature (in this connection Stalin's article stands in the forefront)."* This work was the major Bolshevik pronouncement on the national question in the international arena in the prewar period. *It was a formulation of the Bolshevik theory and program on the national problem.* Two methods, two programs, two outlooks on the national question were sharply contrasted in this work—that of the Second International and that of Leninism. Stalin worked with Lenin to demolish the opportunist views and dogmas of the Second International on this question. It was Lenin and Stalin who worked out

* *Ibid.,* Vol. XVII, p. 116.

the Marxist program on the national problem. Stalin, in this work, presents a Marxist theory of nations, formulates the principles of the Bolshevik solution of the national problem (which demands that it be treated as part of the general problem of the revolution and inseparably from the entire international situation in the era of imperialism), and gives the theoretical foundation of the Bolshevik principle of international working-class solidarity.

On February 23, 1913, Stalin was arrested at an evening arranged by the St. Petersburg Bolshevik Committee in the Kalashnikov Hall. This time the tsarist government exiled Stalin to the remote region of Turukhansk, for a term of four years. At first he lived in the small settlement of Kostino; but, at the beginning of 1914, fearful lest he should escape again, the tsarist gendarmes transferred him still further north, to the settlement of Kureika, on the very fringe of the Arctic Circle, where he lived for three years—1914, 1915 and 1916. Severer conditions of political exile could scarcely have been found in all the remote expanses of the Siberian wilderness.

In the summer of 1914, the imperialist war broke out. The parties of the Second International shamefully betrayed the proletariat and joined the camp of the imperialist bourgeoisie. Only the Bolsheviks, headed by Lenin, remained true to the battle standard of internationalism. Immediately and unhesitatingly, the Bolsheviks, alone of all parties, called for a resolute struggle against the imperialist war. And Stalin, cut off though he was from the outside world and isolated from Lenin and the Party centres, took up the same internationalist stand as Lenin on the questions of war, peace, and revolution. He wrote letters to Lenin. He addressed meetings of exiled Bolsheviks in the village of Monastyrskoye (1915) where he stigmatized the cowardly and treacherous behaviour of Kamenev at the trial of the five Bolshevik members of the Fourth Duma. In 1916, he and other Bolshevik exiles sent a message of greetings to the legally published Bolshevik magazine *Voprosy Strakhovania (Insurance Questions)*, pointing out that it was the duty of this magazine "to devote all its efforts and energies to the ideological insurance of the working class of our country against the deeply corrupting, anti-proletarian preaching of gentry like Potressov, Levitsky and Plekhanov, preaching running directly counter to the principles of internationalism."

In December 1916 Stalin, having been called up to the army, was sent under escort to Krasnoyarsk, and thence to Achinsk. There it was that he heard the first tidings of the revolution of February 1917. In the early part of March 1917, he bade farewell to Achinsk, on the way wiring a message of greetings to Lenin in Switzerland.

On March 12, 1917, Stalin, after all the hardships of exile so bravely endured in Turukhansk, again set foot in Petrograd—the revolutionary capital of Russia. The Central Committee of the Party instructed him to take charge of the *Pravda*.

The Bolshevik Party had just emerged from underground. Many of its most prominent and active members were still on their way back from remote prisons and places of exile. Lenin was abroad, and the bourgeois Provisional Government was putting every obstacle in the way of his return. In this momentous period Stalin worked to rally the Party for the fight for the transition from the bourgeois-democratic revolution to the Socialist revolution. Together with Molotov, he directed the activities of the Central Committee and the Petrograd Committee of the Bolshevik Party. In his articles the Bolsheviks found the guiding principles they needed in their work. The very first article he wrote on his return from exile, "The Soviets of Workers' and Soldiers' Deputies," spoke of the main task of the Party, which, Stalin said, was "to consolidate these Soviets, to form them everywhere, and link them together under a Central Soviet of Workers' and Soldiers' Deputies as the organ of revolutionary power of the people."*

In an article "The War," Stalin showed that the imperialist character of the war had not changed with the assumption of power by the Provisional Government, and that under the bourgeois Provisional

---

* J. V. Stalin, *Collected Works*, Russ. ed., Vol. 3, p. 2.

Government the war of 1914-17 remained a predatory and unjust war.

Stalin, Molotov and others, supported by the majority of the Party members, advocated a policy of "no confidence" in the imperialist Provisional Government, and denounced both the defencism of the Mensheviks and Socialist-Revolutionaries and the semi-Menshevik position of conditional support for the Provisional Government advocated by Kamenev and other opportunists.

★

V

O N APRIL 3, 1917, after a long period of exile, Lenin returned to Russia. The news of the arrival of the beloved leader of the revolution was hailed with enthusiasm by the advanced workers of Petrograd. Stalin, with a delegation of workers, went to meet him at Byelo-Ostrov. The welcome accorded to Lenin upon his arrival at the Finland Railway Terminus in Petrograd turned into a mighty revolutionary demonstration. On the morrow of his arrival, Lenin propounded his famous April Theses. The fruit of Lenin's genius, they provided the Party with a plan of action for the transition from the bourgeois-democratic to the Socialist revolution. They gave the Party a new orientation in the new conditions of the struggle that followed the overthrow of tsardom. On April 24, 1917, the Seventh (April) Conference of the Bolshevik Party assembled. Lenin's theses constituted the basis of its deliberations. The Conference directed the efforts of the Party to the struggle for the transition from the bourgeois-democratic revolution to the Socialist revolution.

At this Conference Stalin vigorously supported Lenin's orientation towards a Socialist revolution and exposed the opportunist, anti-Leninist line of Kamenev, Rykov and their handful of supporters. Stalin also made a report on the national question. Developing a consistent Marxist-Leninist line, he expounded the Bolshevik national policy, advocating the right of nations to self-determination, even to the point of secession and the formation of independent states. It was the national policy of Lenin and Stalin that was to secure for the Party the support of the oppressed nationalities in the Great October Socialist Revolution.

After the Conference, in May 1917, a Political Bureau of the Central Committee was instituted. Stalin was elected a member of the Political Bureau and has been successively re-elected to it ever since.

On the basis of the decisions of the April Conference, the Party set energetically to work to win over the masses, and to train and organize them for militant action.

In this complex period of the revolution, when events moved at breakneck speed, demanding skilful and flexible tactics of the Party, it was Lenin and Stalin who guided the struggle of the masses.

"I recall the year 1917," says Stalin, "when, after my wanderings from one prison and place of exile to another, I was transferred by the will of the Party to Leningrad. There in the society of Russian workers, and in direct contact with Comrade Lenin, the great teacher of the proletarians of all countries, in the midst of the storm of mighty conflicts between the proletariat and the bourgeoisie, in the midst of the imperialist war, I first learnt what it meant to be one of the leaders of the great Party of the working class. There, in the society of Russian workers— the liberators of oppressed peoples and the pioneers of the proletarian struggle in all countries and among all peoples—I received my third revolutionary baptism of fire. There, in Russia, under Lenin's guidance, I became a master of the art of revolution."*

Stalin was at the centre of all the practical activities of the Party. As a member of the Central Committee he took a direct and leading part in the work of the Petrograd Committee of the Party, edited the *Pravda,* wrote articles for it and for the *Soldatskaya Pravda,* and directed the Bolshevik campaign in the Petrograd municipal elections. Together with Lenin, he took part in the All-Russian Conference of the Party Organizations in the Army, where he delivered a report on "The National Movement and the National Regiments." Together with Lenin, he organized the historic demonstration of June 18, which marched under the slogans of the Bolshevik Party; and he drew up the Manifesto of the Central Committee to the workers and revolutionary soldiers of Petrograd. On June 20 the First

* J. V. Stalin, *Collected Works,* Russ. ed., Vol. 8, p. 175.

All-Russian Congress of Soviets elected Stalin to the Central Executive Committee.

After the events of July 1917, when Lenin, hounded and persecuted by the counter-revolutionary Provisional Government, was forced to go into hiding, Stalin directly guided the work of the Central Committee and the Central Party Organ, which at that time appeared under a succession of different names (*Rabochy i Soldat, Proletary, Rabochy, Rabochy Put*). It was Stalin who saved the precious life of Lenin for the Party, for the Soviet people and for all humanity, by vigorously resisting the proposal of the traitors Kamenev, Rykov and Trotsky that Lenin should appear for trial before the courts of the counter-revolutionary Provisional Government.

The brutal suppression of the July demonstration marked a turning point in the development of the revolution. Lenin worked out new tactics for the Party in the new conditions of the struggle. Together with Sverdlov, Stalin steered the work of the Sixth Party Congress (July-August 1917), which had to meet secretly. At this Congress Stalin made the report on the work of the Central Committee and a report on the political situation, in which he gave a clear-cut formulation of the tasks and tactics of the Party in the struggle for the Socialist revolution. He rebutted the Trotskyites, who held that Socialism could not be victorious in Russia.

Opposing the attempt of the Trotskyites to make the Party's orientation towards Socialist revolution contingent on a proletarian revolution in the West, Comrade Stalin declared: "The possibility is not excluded that Russia will be the country that will lay the road to Socialism.... We must discard the antiquated idea that only Europe can show us the way. There is dogmatic Marxism and creative Marxism. I stand by the latter."* Stalin's words were prophetic. Russia was the first to show the way to Socialism.

In insisting on Lenin's doctrine that the victory of Socialism was possible in Russia, Stalin had the full support of the Congress. Guided by Stalin and by Lenin's instructions, the Sixth Congress inaugurated the preparations for insurrection. The Congress headed the Party for armed insurrection and for the establishment of the dictatorship of the proletariat.

In August 1917, General Kornilov launched his revolt with the aim of restoring tsardom in Russia. The Bolsheviks roused the masses to resist the attempted coup, and the Kornilov revolt was crushed. This ushered in a new phase in the history of the revolution: the phase of organization for the grand assault.

While Lenin was in hiding Stalin maintained a correspondence with his teacher and friend and kept

* J. V. Stalin, *Collected Works*, Russ. ed., Vol. 3, pp. 186, 187.

in close contact with him. He visited him twice in his place of concealment near Razliv.

Boldly and confidently, firmly yet circumspectly, Lenin and Stalin led the Party and the working class towards the Socialist revolution, towards armed insurrection. It was they who inspired and organized the victory of the Great October Socialist Revolution. Stalin was Lenin's closest associate. He had direct charge of all the preparations for the insurrection. His articles in the central press laying down the guiding policy were reprinted in the provincial Bolshevik newspapers. He summoned representatives from the regional organizations to Petrograd, gave them instructions and outlined plans of campaign for the various regions. On October 16, the Central Committee elected a Party Centre, headed by Comrade Stalin, to direct the uprising. This Centre was the leading core of the Revolutionary Military Committee of the Petrograd Soviet and had practical direction of the whole uprising.

At the meeting of the Central Committee of the Party on October 16, Stalin rebuffed the capitulatory proposals of the traitors Zinoviev and Kamenev, who opposed armed insurrection. "Objectively," he declared, "what Kamenev and Zinoviev propose would enable the counter-revolution to prepare and organize. We would be retreating without end and would lose the revolution. Why should we not insure for ourselves the possibility of choosing the day and the conditions for the uprising, so as to deprive the counter-revolution of the possibility of organizing?"*

Early in the morning of October 24, Kerensky ordered the suppression of the central organ of the Party, *Rabochy Put*, and sent a number of armoured cars to the editorial and printing offices of the newspaper. But by 10 a.m. a force of Red Guards and revolutionary soldiers, acting on Comrade Stalin's instructions, had pressed back the armoured cars and placed a strong guard over the printing and editorial offices. At eleven o'clock the *Rabochy Put* came out, with a leading article by Stalin enti-tled "What Do We Need?" calling upon the masses to overthrow the bourgeois Provisional Government. At the same time, on instructions of the Party Cen-tre, detachments of revolutionary soldiers and Red Guards were rushed to the Smolny Institute. The insurrection began on October 24. On the evening of October 25 the Second Congress of Soviets met and turned over the government power to the Soviets.

Stalin was a member of the first Council of People's Commissars, which, headed by Lenin, was set up by the Second All-Russian Congress of Soviets after the victory of the October Revolution.

The Great October Socialist Revolution ushered

---

* J. V. Stalin, *Collected Works*, Russ. ed., Vol. 3, p. 381.

in changes of momentous importance. It split the world into two systems—capitalist and Socialist. The Bolshevik Party was now faced with new conditions, with new gigantic tasks. And the forms of struggle of the working class likewise underwent a fundamental change.

From the inception of the Soviet Government and down to 1923, Stalin was the People's Commissar for the Affairs of the Nationalities. He personally directed all the measures taken by the Party and the Soviet Government to solve the national problem in the U.S.S.R. Guided by Lenin and Stalin, the workers and peasants began to turn the tsarist colonies into Soviet republics. There is not a single Soviet republic in whose organization Stalin did not take an active and leading part. He directed the fight for the formation of the Ukrainian Soviet Republic, the Byelorussian Republic and the Soviet republics of Transcaucasia and Central Asia, and he helped the numerous nationalities of the Soviet Land to set up their autonomous republics and regions. Lenin and Stalin were the inspirers and organizers of the great Union of Soviet Socialist Republics.

Lenin's closest assistants in the organization of the Soviet state were Stalin and Sverdlov. Stalin fought side by side with Lenin against Kamenev, Zinoviev, Rykov and the other scabs and deserters from the revolution. He took an active and leading part in all decisive measures and actions, such as the organization of the defeat of Kerensky and Krasnov, the breaking of the sabotage of the old government officials, the liquidation of the counter-revolutionary General Headquarters and the removal of the tsarist generals, the suppression of the bourgeois press, the fight against the counter-revolutionary Ukrainian Rada, the dispersal of the Constituent Assembly, and the drafting of the first Soviet Constitution in 1918.

In January 1918, on the instructions of the Central Committee, Stalin arranged a conference of representatives of the revolutionary wings of the Socialist parties of Europe and America, which was an important step towards the formation of the Third, Communist International.

In the trying days of the Brest-Litovsk negotiations, when the fate of the revolution hung in the balance, Stalin was at one with Lenin in upholding the Bolshevik strategy and tactics against the traitor Trotsky and his henchman Bukharin, who, in conjunction with the British and French imperialists, sought to expose the young and still weak Soviet Republic to the blows of German imperialism.

★

VI

OVERTHROWN by the October Socialist Revolution, the Russian landlords and capitalists began to conspire with the capitalists of other countries for the organization of military intervention against the Land of the Soviets, with the aim of defeating the workers and peasants, overthrowing the Soviet regime and once again fastening the chains of slavery on the country. Civil War and intervention began. The Soviet Government proclaimed the Socialist fatherland in danger and called upon the people to rise in its defence. The Bolshevik Party rallied the workers and peasants for a *patriotic* war against the foreign invaders and the bourgeois and landlord Whiteguards.

In the spring of 1918, the British and French imperialists instigated a revolt of the Czechoslovak Corps (formed of prisoners of war from the Austro-Hungarian army) which, after the conclusion of peace with Germany, was making its way to France via Siberia.

The revolt of the Czechoslovaks, which was timed to coincide with the revolts engineered by Whiteguards and Socialist-Revolutionaries in twenty-three cities on the Volga, a revolt of the Left Socialist-Revolutionaries in Moscow, and a landing of British troops in Murmansk, unleashed all the forces of counter-revolution. The moment was a highly critical one. The country had only just torn itself from the clutches of the imperialist war. The misrule of the capitalists and landlords had brought the country to the verge of disaster. The workers in Moscow and Petrograd were receiving a bare two ounces of bread a day. The republic was cut off from the granaries of the Ukraine and Siberia. The southeast, the Volga region and the North Caucasus, was the only area from which grain could still be obtained, and the road to them lay by way of the Volga, through Tsaritsyn. Only by procuring grain could the revolution be saved. Lenin appealed to the workers of Petrograd to organize expeditions into the country-side to help the poor peasants against the grain profiteers, kulaks and usurers.

Stalin left for the South, invested by the Central Committee with extraordinary powers to direct the mobilization of food supplies in the south of Russia. On June 6, 1918, Stalin arrived in Tsaritsyn with a detachment of workers. Combining as he did the insight of a political leader with the talent of a military strategist, Stalin at once realized the importance of Tsaritsyn, as the point of main attack of the counter-revolutionary forces. The capture of Tsaritsyn would have cut off the republic from its last sources of grain supply and from the oil of Baku, and would have enabled the Whites to link the counter-revolution in the Don region with Kolchak and the Czechoslovak counter-revolution for a general advance on Moscow. Tsaritsyn had to be retained for the Soviet State at all costs.

After clearing the city of Whiteguard plotters with a stern hand and securing and dispatching substantial supplies of food to the starving capitals, Stalin turned his whole attention to the defence of Tsaritsyn. He ruthlessly broke down the resistance of the counter-revolutionary military experts appointed and supported by Trotsky, and took swift and vigorous measures to reorganize the scattered detachments and to expedite the arrival from the Donbas of Voroshilov's units, which subsequently formed the nucleus of the Tenth Army. Stalin's iron will and foresight of genius saved Tsaritsyn and prevented the Whites from breaking through to Moscow.

The epic defence of Tsaritsyn coincided with the debacle of German imperialism in the Ukraine. In November 1918, revolution broke out in Germany and Austria-Hungary. The Central Committee commissioned Stalin to organize the Ukrainian Front and assist the Ukrainian workers and peasants. Twenty leading Party workers from the Tenth Army, headed by Comrade Voroshilov, were placed at his disposal. At the end of November the Ukrainian insurrectionary troops advanced against Petlura and the Germans and liberated Kharkov. Minsk, in the West, was also liberated. Stalin performed inestimable service in the liberation of the Western regions and the formation of the Byelorussian Republic.

On November 30, 1918, a Council of Workers' and Peasants' Defence was set up, headed by Lenin, to direct the entire work of defence, both at the front and in the rear, and to mobilize the industries, the transport system and all the resources of the country. Stalin was appointed to the Council of Defence as the representative of the All-Russian Central Executive Committee, and virtually acted as Lenin's deputy.

At the end of 1918 the situation became catastrophic on the Eastern Front. Kolchak's army was hastening to join forces with the British troops that were advancing from the North. Acting in the name of the Council of Defence, Lenin demanded that steps be taken to strengthen the position at Perm. He proposed that the Central Committee appoint Stalin and Dzerzhinsky to avert the threatened disaster. Arrived at the Perm Front, Stalin acted swiftly and drastically, and soon had the situation in hand. In the South, at Tsaritsyn, his iron will had prevented the counter-revolutionaries of the Don from joining forces with the counter-revolutionaries of the Urals and the Volga. In the North, he frustrated the attempt of the forces of intervention to effect a junction with the Czechs and Kolchak. Cut off from his allies in the South and in the North, Kolchak was soon in full retreat before the Red forces.

Returning from the Eastern Front, Stalin addressed himself to the task of organizing the State Control, and, in March 1919, on Lenin's nomination, was appointed People's Commissar of the State Control, which body was later reorganized into the People's Commissariat of Workers' and Peasants' Inspection. In this post he remained until April 1922, performing inestimable service in the cause of enlisting the working people in the work of administering the state.

In May 1919, General Yudenich, with the support of the Finnish Whites and of Estonian troops, started a swift advance on Petrograd, with the aim of diverting the Red forces from Kolchak. This offensive was supported by a British naval squadron. A mutiny of the forts of Krasnaya Gorka and Seraya Loshad was engineered in the rear of the Red Army. The Red front wavered, and the enemy broke through to the very gates of Petrograd.

The Central Committee chose Stalin to organize the resistance to the Whites. Communists poured to the front. Stalin soon stopped the disarray. making short work of enemies and traitors. The mutinous forts were captured by a combined blow from land and sea, and the White troops were hurled back. The threat to Petrograd was removed. The plans of the Entente to capture that city were frustrated.

Yudenich was routed, the remnants of his army taking refuge in Estonia.

In the summer of 1919, Stalin went to Smolensk, on the Western Front, to organize the resistance to the Polish offensive.

Beaten in this first campaign, the Entente, after having crushed the Soviets in Bavaria, Hungary, Estonia and Latvia, launched a new campaign in the autumn of 1919, enlisting, besides their own and White troops, the armies of the small states bordering on Russia. Winston Churchill, then British Secretary for War, braggingly referred to this attempt as "the campaign of fourteen states."

While the Red Army was engaged in routing Kolchak in the East, Denikin seized the Donets Basin and invaded the Ukraine along a broad front. Trotsky's treacherous activities had disorganized the Southern Front, and the Red forces sustained defeat after defeat. The Polish Whites came to the aid of Denikin and captured Minsk. Yudenich launched a new offensive against Petrograd, while Kolchak tried to make a stand on the Tobol. Denikin's advanced units captured Oryol and were approaching Tula. Never had the enemy been within such close reach of the Soviet capital. The Donets capitalists even offered a reward of a million rubles to the first White regiment to enter Moscow.

In face of this White offensive, Lenin issued an impassioned appeal on behalf of the Central Committee to all the Party organizations. "All for the fight against Denikin!" was his cry.

Mass reinforcements and munitions were rushed to the Southern Front. But a leader was needed to weld together the hundreds of thousands of men, to cement them by a single will and hurl them against the enemy. In September 1919, the Central Committee sent Stalin to organize victory on the Southern Front.

Confusion, disarray and a total lack of strategical plan was what this military leader of the revolution found when he arrived at the front. He cleared the staffs of Trotsky's discredited placemen and demanded that Trotsky be not allowed under any circumstances to interfere in the affairs of the front. He scrapped the old criminal plan which proposed to break through Denikin's line by an advance from the Volga (Tsaritsyn) to Novorossiisk, and drew up a plan of combat of his own, which was a stroke of strategical genius. He proposed that the main thrust be made against Denikin from the Voronezh area through Kharkov, the Donets Basin, and Rostov, so as to cut the counter-revolutionary army in two. This plan would ensure the rapid advance of the Red Army, as the line of march lay through proletarian centres where the population was in open sympathy with the Red Army and impatiently awaiting its arrival, and where there was an extensive network of railways which would enable the troops to receive all necessary supplies. At the same time this plan would free the Donbas—with its vast coal fields—which would be a source of fuel for the country and a reservoir of revolutionary forces.

Stalin's plan was approved by the Central Committee.

Stalin worked might and main to organize victory. He intently followed the operations, correcting mistakes as they arose, selected the commanders and political workers, and imbued them with his own fighting spirit. Under Stalin's direction, instructions for regimental commissars on the Southern Front were drawn up, in which their duties were defined in the following striking words:

"The regimental commissar is the political and moral leader of his regiment, the first to defend its material and spiritual interests. While the regimental commander is the head of the regiment, the commissar is its father and its soul."*

Thanks to Stalin's plan, Denikin was completely routed. It was on Stalin's initiative that the glorious First Mounted Army was formed, which, commanded by Budyonny, Voroshilov and Shchadenko and supported by the other armies on the Southern Front, gave the coup de grâce to Denikin's forces.

During the brief respite that the Soviet Republic received after the defeat of Denikin, Lenin placed

---

* *Pravda*, No. 344, December 14, 1939 (Editorial "Military Commissars").

V. I. Lenin, J. V. Stalin and M. I. Kalinin at the Eighth Congress of the Russian Communist Party (Bolsheviks), March 1919

Photo

Stalin in charge of restoring the war-devastated economy of the Ukraine. In February and March 1920 he headed the Council of the Ukrainian labour army and mobilized the working people for the fight for coal. At this moment "coal is just as important for Russia as the victory over Denikin was,"* he said, in an address to the labour army in March 1920. And under Stalin's guidance the Ukrainian Bolsheviks registered substantial achievements in supplying the country with fuel and improving the work of the railways.

In May 1920, the Central Committee commissioned Stalin to the South-Western Front against the Polish Whites, who formed the spearhead of the third Entente campaign against the Soviet Republic. Here Stalin took a personal part in directing the operations that broke the Polish Front and led to the liberation of Kiev and the advance of the Soviet troops to Lvov. In the same year Stalin organized the defence of the southern Ukraine against Wrangel, and outlined a plan for the destruction of his forces. Stalin's recommendations formed the basis of Frunze's plan of operations which resulted in Wrangel's utter defeat.

Through all these years of civil war Lenin and Stalin worked in the closest collaboration. Acting hand in hand, they built up and strengthened the

---

* J. V. Stalin, *Collected Works*, Russ. ed., Vol. 4, p. 293.

Red Army. Lenin consulted Stalin on all major questions of Soviet policy and on military strategy and tactics. When Stalin was in remote parts of the country fulfilling important political and military missions assigned to him by Lenin, they kept up a constant correspondence by letters, notes and telegrams. Stalin kept Lenin systematically informed of the situation at the fronts. In his letters and telegrams he gave masterly analyses of the military situation. He invariably turned to Lenin for assistance and support whenever conditions at the front became particularly precarious. Lenin was always extremely attentive to Stalin's requests. He kept him constantly informed of developments and shared with him political news. Stalin was Lenin's chief mainstay in the organization and direction of the defence of the Soviet Republic.

During the Civil War the Central Committee of the Party, and Lenin personally, sent Stalin to the most crucial fronts, wherever the threat to the revolution was most imminent. Comrade Stalin was a member of the Revolutionary Military Council of the Republic and of the Revolutionary Military Councils of the Western, Southern and South-Western Fronts. Wherever, for various reasons, the Red Army found itself in mortal danger, wherever the advance of the armies of counter-revolution and intervention threatened the very existence of the Soviet regime, there Stalin was sent. "Wherever confusion and panic might at any moment develop into helplessness and catastrophe," writes Voroshilov, "there Comrade Stalin was always sure to appear."*

And wherever he went, Stalin would organize the Party rank and file and the worker masses, and firmly take the reins of leadership into his hands. Relying on the support of the masses, he would ruthlessly crush all sabotage, suppress with an iron hand the conspiracies of traitors and spies in the rear and at the front. By his personal example, by his selfless labour and clear revolutionary perspective, he would rouse the fighting spirit and revolutionary enthusiasm of workers, peasants, Red Army men, swiftly securing a radical change in the situation and victory for the Red Army.

He saw through and foiled the most artful and insidious strategic plans of the enemy, confounding their military "science," "art" and training.

Stalin's services in the Civil War received special recognition in a decision adopted by the All-Russian Central Executive Committee, on Lenin's motion, on November 27, 1919, awarding him the Order of the Red Banner.

It was the Bolshevik Party, headed by Lenin and Stalin, that created the Red Army—the first Red Army in the world, the army of the emancipated

---

* K. E. Voroshilov, *Stalin and the Red Army*, Russ. ed., 1940, pp. 6-7.

workers and peasants, of the brotherhood of the peoples of the Soviet country, an army educated in the spirit of internationalism. Lenin and Stalin it was who, with other outstanding leaders of the Bolshevik Party, directed the defence of the country.

It was Stalin who directly inspired and organized the major victories of the Red Army. Wherever the destinies of the revolution were being decided in battle, there the Party sent Stalin. It was he who drew up the most important strategical plans and who directed the decisive military operations. At Tsaritsyn and Perm, at Petrograd and in the operations against Denikin, in the West against the Polish gentry and in the South against Wrangel, everywhere Stalin's iron will and strategical genius ensured victory for the revolution. Stalin it was who trained and directed the military commissars, without whom, as Lenin said, there would have been no Red Army.

With Stalin's name are linked the most glorious victories of our Red Army.

★

VIII

AVING VICTORIOUSLY ended the war against the forces of intervention, the Soviet government turned to the work of peaceful economic development. Four years of imperialist war and three years of civil war had reduced the country to a state of ruin. The Civil War over, the peasants began to voice discontent at the levying of all their surplus produce under the surplus-appropriation system, and to demand a sufficient supply of manufactured goods. Due to hunger and fatigue, a section of the workers, too, began to show signs of discontent. The class enemy tried to turn the dire economic distress of the country to his own ends.

The Party was confronted with the necessity of working out a new line of policy on all questions affecting the economic life of the country. It was clear to the Central Committee that, the war over and peaceful economic development having begun, the system of War Communism no longer served its purpose. The need for the surplus-appropriation system had passed, and it was now necessary to allow the peasants to dispose of the greater part of their surplus produce at their own discretion. This would make it possible to revive agriculture and trade, to restore industry, to improve supplies to the towns and to create a new foundation, an economic foundation, for the alliance of the workers and peasants.

But there were groups within the Party that tried to obstruct the adoption of the new policies. At the end of 1920, these anti-Party groups forced a controversy on the Party, known as the discussion on the trade unions. Actually this discussion was of much broader import than the question of the trade unions. The real point at issue was the policy to be adopted towards the peasantry, the policy of the Party towards the masses of non-Party workers, and the Party's approach in the new situation to the masses generally. The Trotskyites proposed "tightening the screws" of War Communism. Their treasonable policy of sheer coercion and dictation was designed to set the non-Party worker masses against the Party, and to endanger the very existence of the Soviet system. Their lead was followed by other anti-Party groups, such as the "Workers' Opposition," the "Democratic Centralists" and the "Left Communists."

Shoulder to shoulder with Lenin, Stalin consistently pursued and upheld the Party line and hit hard at all these enemies of the Party. He directed the organization of the fight against the anti-Leninist groups during the trade union discussion, rallying the Party around Lenin's platform. It was Stalin who received the reports on the progress of the fight for the Party line in the various localities. It was he who sent regular reports to the *Pravda* on the results of the discussion in the local organizations, results which signalized a victory for the Party and the defeat of the anti-Leninist groups.

An important factor in securing the victory of the Party line and in rallying the Party around Lenin and the Leninist majority on the Central Committee was the publication in *Pravda*, on January 19, 1921, of Stalin's article, "Our Differences." Lenin and Stalin together upheld the unity of the Party against all attacks of the anti-Party factions and groups.

Thus, it was united on Lenin's principles that the Party came to its Tenth Congress, which met in March 1921, to discuss the fundamental problems involved in the further victorious advance of the revolution. The Congress summed up the discussion on the trade unions and by an overwhelming majority endorsed Lenin's platform. It adopted the momentous decision to replace the surplus-appropriation system by a tax in kind, and to introduce the New Economic Policy, of which Lenin was the author and inspiration. The decision of the Tenth Congress on the adoption of the New Economic Policy ensured a durable alliance of the working class and the peasantry for the building of Socialism.

This same prime object was served by the decision of the Congress on the national question. The report on "The Immediate Tasks of the Party in Connection with the National Problem" was made by Stalin.

Stalin's report, and the Congress resolution, gave a clear and precise formulation of the basic practical tasks in regard to the national problem. We had abolished national oppression, Stalin declared, but that was not enough. The evil heritage of the past had to be abolished—the economic, political and cultural backwardness of the formerly oppressed peoples; they had to be helped to catch up with Central Russia in these fields. Stalin called upon the Party to combat dominant-nation chauvinism, Great-Russian chauvinism, which was the chief danger, and likewise local nationalism.

A year of NEP passed. At its Eleventh Congress (March-April 1922) the Party reviewed the results of the first year of the New Economic Policy. These results were such as to entitle Lenin to declare at the Congress:

"For a year we have been retreating. In the name of the Party we must now call a halt. The purpose pursued by the retreat has been achieved. This period is drawing, or has drawn, to a close. Now our purpose is different—to regroup our forces."*

* V. I. Lenin, *Collected Works*, 3rd Russ. ed., Vol. XXVII, p. 238.

V. I. Lenin and J. V. Stalin in Gorki, 1922
Photo

The historic tasks set by Lenin at the Congress had now to be carried out. On Lenin's motion, the Plenum of the Central Committee, on April 3, 1922, elected Stalin, Lenin's best and most faithful disciple and associate, General Secretary of the Central Committee, a post at which he has remained ever since.

The wound sustained by Lenin in the attempt made on his life in 1918, and the constant strain of overwork, undermined his health and from the end of 1921 he was forced to absent himself from his work more and more frequently. The main burden of the work of guiding the affairs of the Party fell upon the shoulders of Stalin.

At this period Stalin performed an immense task in the forming of the national Soviet republics, and then in the amalgamation of all the Soviet republics into one union state—the U.S.S.R. On December 30, 1922, the First All-Union Congress of Soviets, on the motion of Lenin and Stalin, passed the historic decision on the voluntary amalgamation of the Soviet nations to form the Union of Soviet Socialist Republics—the U.S.S.R. Speaking at the Congress Stalin said:

"This day marks a turning point in the history of the Soviet government. It places a landmark between the old period, now past, when the Soviet republics, although they acted in common, yet each followed its own path and was concerned primarily with its own preservation, and the new period, already begun, when an end is being put to the isolated existence of the various Soviet republics, when the republics are being amalgamated into a single federal state in order successfully to cope with economic disruption, and when the Soviet government is concerned not only with its preservation, but with developing into an important international power, capable of influencing the international situation and of modifying it in the interests of the toilers."*

The formation of the U.S.S.R. was a big victory for the national policy of Lenin and Stalin. The Soviet Union was built on the unshakable foundation of the confidence in the great Russian nation conceived by the peoples formerly oppressed by tsardom, on the firm foundation of the mutual friendship of the peoples of the Soviet Land.

In April 1923 the Party held its Twelfth Congress. This was the first congress since the victory of the October Socialist Revolution that Lenin did not attend, being prevented by illness. All the recommendations made by Lenin in his latest articles and letters were embodied in its decisions. The Congress administered a vigorous rebuff to those who sought to represent NEP as a retreat from Socialist principles and who would have the country place itself

---

* J. V. Stalin, *Collected Works*, Russ. ed., Vol. 5, p. 156.

in bondage to capitalism. It condemned the treacherous and capitulatory proposals of the Trotskyites
and Bukharinites.

At this Congress Stalin made the report on the
organization work of the Central Committee, and
another on "National Factors in Party and State
Development." In the first report he gave a broad
picture of the Party's activities, of its growth, and
of the growing strength of the transmission belts
from the Party to the masses (the trade unions, the
Y.C.L., the Soviets, etc.), reviewed the results of the
two years of NEP and indicated the lines of further
development. Concluding his report, Stalin said:
"Our Party has remained solid and united; it has
stood the test of a momentous turn, and is marching
on with flying colours."*

The national question was one of the principal
items at the Congress. In his report on this question Stalin stressed the tremendous international
significance of our national policy, and pointed out
that the oppressed nations of the East and West
looked on the Soviet Union as a model solution of the
national problem. He said that energetic measures
were needed to put an end to economic and cultural inequality among the peoples of the Soviet
Union, and called upon the Party to put up a determined fight against Great-Russian chauvinism and

* *Ibid.*, p. 222.

local nationalism, which had gained ground with the partial revival of capitalism. He denounced the Georgian nationalist deviators, who were being supported by the Trotskyites.

Hardly had the Twelfth Party Congress come to a close when a serious menace to the Soviet Republic loomed on the horizon. The arch-reactionary and interventionist elements of the bourgeoisie who had come to power in Britain and France, tried to organize a new crusade against the Soviet Union. But under Stalin's leadership the Party emerged from this critical situation with flying colours and gained a resounding victory on the diplomatic front. By 1924 all the bigger European capitalist states had changed their tune from threats and ultimatums to recognition of the U.S.S.R. "The fact that we emerged from our difficulties then without detriment to our cause," Stalin said later, "undoubtedly shows that Comrade Lenin's disciples had already learned a thing or two from their master."*

The Thirteenth Party Conference met in January 1924. Stalin delivered a report reviewing the discussion. The Trotskyites received severe condemnation from the Conference. Its decisions were endorsed by the Thirteenth Party Congress (May 1924 and the Fifth Congress of the Comintern (summer, 1924).

---

* J. V. Stalin, *Collected Works*, Russ. ed., Vol. 6, p. 36.

On January 21, 1924, Lenin, the leader and founder of the Bolshevik Party, the leader of the working people of the whole world, passed away in the village of Gorki, near Moscow. The banner of Lenin, the banner of the Party, was taken up and carried on by Lenin's distinguished disciple, Stalin—the finest son of the Bolshevik Party, Lenin's worthy successor and the great continuator of his cause.

At a meeting of mourning of the Second All-Union Congress of Soviets, which met on January 26, Stalin made a solemn vow in the name of the Party:

"We Communists are people of a special mould. We are made of a special stuff. We are those who form the army of the great proletarian strategist, the army of Comrade Lenin. There is nothing higher than the honour of belonging to this army. There is nothing higher than the title of member of the Party whose founder and leader is Comrade Lenin. . . .

"Departing from us, Comrade Lenin adjured us to hold high and guard the purity of the great title of member of the Party. We vow to you, Comrade Lenin, that we will fulfil your behest with credit! . . .

"Departing from us, Comrade Lenin adjured us to guard the unity of our Party as the apple of our eye. We vow to you, Comrade Lenin, that this behest, too, we will fulfil with credit! . . .

"Departing from us, Comrade Lenin adjured us to guard and strengthen the dictatorship of the proletariat. We vow to you, Comrade Lenin, that we will spare no effort to fulfil this behest, too, with credit! . . .

"Departing from us, Comrade Lenin adjured us to strengthen with all our might the alliance of the workers and the peasants. We vow to you, Comrade Lenin, that this behest, too, we will fulfil with credit! . . .

"Comrade Lenin untiringly urged upon us the necessity of maintaining the voluntary union of the nations of our country, the necessity for fraternal cooperation between them within the framework of the Union of Republics.

"Departing from us, Comrade Lenin adjured us to consolidate and extend the Union of Republics. We vow to you, Comrade Lenin, that this behest, too, we will fulfil with credit! . . .

"More than once did Lenin point out to us that the strengthening of the Red Army and the improvement of its condition is one of the most important tasks of our Party. . . . Let us vow then, comrades, that we will spare no effort to strengthen our Red Army and our Red Navy! . . .

"Departing from us, Comrade Lenin adjured us to remain faithful to the principles of the Communist International. We vow to you, Comrade Lenin, that we will not spare our lives to

80

strengthen and extend the union of the toilers of the whole world—the Communist International...".

This was a vow of the Bolshevik Party to its teacher and leader, Lenin, whose memory will live through the ages. And under Stalin's leadership, the Party has faithfully adhered to its vow.

On the first anniversary of Lenin's death, Stalin wrote the following in a letter to the newspaper *Rabochaya Gazeta*:

"Remember, love and study Lenin, our teacher and leader.

"Fight and vanquish the enemies, internal and foreign—as Lenin taught us.

"Build the new life, the new way of existence, the new culture—as Lenin taught us.

"Never refuse to do the little things, for from little things are built the big things—this is one of Lenin's important behests."**

The Soviet people have unswervingly followed these precepts of Stalin.

The enemies of Socialism took advantage of Lenin's illness and then of his death to try to deflect the Party from the Leninist path and thus pave the way for the restoration of capitalism in the Soviet Union. Foremost in these attacks on the Party were

---

* J. V. Stalin, *Collected Works*, Russ. ed., Vol. 6, pp. 46-51.
** *Ibid.*, Vol. 7, p. 15.

81

Trotsky, that arch-enemy of Leninism, and his henchmen. The Trotskyites forced a new discussion on the Party. In the bitter fight that ensued, Stalin laid bare the political meaning of the Trotskyites' attacks and showed that it was the life and death of the Party that was at stake. He mustered the Party forces for the defeat of Trotskyism.

"It is the duty of the Party to *bury Trotskyism as an ideological trend*," said Stalin in his speech, "Trotskyism or Leninism," at a meeting of the Party members on the All-Union Central Council of Trade Unions in November 1924. He made it clear to the Party that in the then existing conditions Trotskyism was the chief danger.

"Today," he declared, "after the victory of the October Revolution, under the present conditions of NEP, Trotskyism must be regarded as the most dangerous trend, for it strives to instil a lack of faith in the forces of our revolution, a lack of faith in the alliance of the workers and peasants, a lack of faith in the conversion of NEP Russia into a Socialist Russia."*

Stalin made it clear that unless Trotskyism was ideologically routed, the continuation of the victorious advance towards Socialism could not be ensured.

"Unless Trotskyism is defeated," he declared, "it will be impossible to achieve victory under the con-

* J. V. Stalin, *Collected Works*, Russ. ed., Vol. 7, pp. 32-33

ditions of NEP, it will be impossible to convert present-day Russia into a Socialist Russia."*

In the battles against Trotskyism, Stalin rallied the Party around the Central Committee and mobilized it to continue the struggle for the victory of Socialism in our country.

Stalin's theoretical work, *The Foundations of Leninism*, published in 1924, played an exceptionally big part in the ideological demolition of Trotskyism, and in defending, explaining and developing Leninism. A masterly exposition and profound theoretical substantiation of Leninism, it armed the Bolsheviks, as it arms them today all over the world, with the trenchant weapon of Marxist-Leninist theory.

This work explains the fundamental principles of Leninism, that is, everything new and distinctive associated with the name of Lenin, everything that he contributed to the development of Marxist theory. The mere fact that the problems of Leninism had been thus generalized, that Lenin's entire ideological legacy had been systematized and examined from the angle of the new epoch in history, was in itself a tremendous stride in the development of the science of Marxism-Leninism. In this work Stalin deals with every aspect of Lenin's teachings on a high theoretical level. We are given a classical definition of Leninism, and are shown how Lenin developed

---

* *Ibid.*

Marxism in conformity with the conditions of a new era, the era of imperialism and proletarian revolutions.

The restoration of the national economy was nearing completion. Both the international situation and conditions at home, in the Soviet Union, had changed. In the capitalist countries a temporary ebb in the tide of revolution and a temporary, partial stabilization of capitalism had set in. In the U.S.S.R. the prewar economic level had been reached. It was now necessary to advance farther. And the question arose in all its urgency—what were the prospects for our further development, what would be the destiny of Socialism in the Soviet Union?

With the farsightedness of genius, Stalin defined these prospects and mapped the definite paths for the further development of the revolution.

"My wish for the workers of Dynamo, and for the workers of all Russia," he wrote in 1924, "is that our industry may forge ahead, that the number of proletarians in Russia may increase in the near future to twenty or thirty million, that collective farming in the countryside may thrive and bring individual farming under its influence, that a highly-developed industry and collective farming may finally weld the proletarians of the factories and the labourers of the soil into a single Socialist army...."*

---

* J. V. Stalin, *Collected Works*, Russ. ed., Vol. 6, p. 321.

Stalin drew general theoretical conclusions from the experience of the Great October Socialist Revolution, the experience of the first years of Socialist construction in the midst of a capitalist encirclement, and upheld and developed Lenin's doctrine of the victory of Socialism in one country.

In December 1924 appeared Stalin's widely-known work, "The October Revolution and the Tactics of the Russian Communists," in which, explaining and substantiating Lenin's thesis regarding the victory of Socialism in one country, he showed that this question must be viewed from two aspects: the domestic and the international. The domestic aspect involved the class relations within the country that was building Socialism; the international aspect involved the relations between the U.S.S.R.—so far the only Socialist country—and the surrounding capitalist world. The workers and peasants of the U.S.S.R. were fully capable of coping with the internal difficulties; they were fully capable of vanquishing their own bourgeoisie economically and building up a complete Socialist society. But so long as the country was surrounded by a capitalist world, the danger of capitalist intervention and of the restoration of capitalism in the U.S.S.R. would persist. In order to eliminate this danger, it would be necessary to destroy the capitalist encirclement, and that could result only from a victorious proletarian revolution in at least several countries. Only then could the victory of Socialism in the U.S.S.R. be considered complete and final.

These theses of Stalin were embodied in the historic resolution of the Fourteenth Party Conference (April 1925), which endorsed the Lenin-Stalin line of working for the victory of Socialism in the U.S.S.R. as a law of the Party, binding on all its members.

Reporting to a meeting of active workers of the Moscow Party organization on "The Work of the Fourteenth Conference of the Russian Communist Party (Bolsheviks)," Stalin stressed the necessity of drawing the middle peasants into the work of building Socialism:

"The main task at present is to rally the middle peasants around the proletariat, to win them over to our side again. The main task at present is to link up with the main masses of the peasantry, to raise their material and cultural level, and to move forward together with these main masses along the road to Socialism. The main task is to build Socialism together with the peasantry, absolutely together with the peasantry, and absolutely under the leadership of the working class, for the leadership of the working class is the fundamental guarantee that our work of construction will proceed along the path of Socialism."*

* J. V. Stalin, *Collected Works*, Russ. ed., Vol. 7, pp. 123-24.

In December 1925 the Party held its Fourteenth Congress. In the political report which Stalin delivered on behalf of the Central Committee, he drew a vivid picture of the growing political and economic might of the Soviet Union. But, he said, we could not content ourselves with these achievements, for our country was still a backward, agrarian country. In order to ensure the economic independence of our country and strengthen its defensive power, and in order to create the necessary economic base for the victory of Socialism, our country had to be converted from an agrarian into an industrial country.

Addressing the Fourteenth Congress, the leader of the Party declared:

"The conversion of our country from an agrarian into an industrial country able to produce the machinery it needs by its own efforts—that is the essence, the basis of our general line."*

The capitulators, Zinoviev and Kamenev, tried to oppose Stalin's plan of Socialist industrialization with a "plan" of their own, under which the U.S.S.R. was to remain an agrarian country. This was a treacherous scheme to enslave the U.S.S.R. and deliver it, bound hand and foot, to the imperialist vultures.

Stalin tore the mask from these despicable capitulators and exposed their Trotskyite-Menshevik souls.

---

* *Ibid.*, p. 355.

The prime task of the Party, Stalin emphasized at the Fourteenth Congress, was to ensure a durable alliance between the working class and the middle peasantry for the construction of Socialism.

The Congress endorsed Socialist industrialization and the fight for the victory of Socialism in the U.S.S.R. as the fundamental task of the Party.

Shortly after the Congress, at the beginning of 1926, Stalin published his book, *On the Problems of Leninism*. In this historic work, he demolished the Zinovievite "philosophy" of liquidation and capitulation and proved that the policy adopted by the Fourteenth Party Congress, namely, the Socialist industrialization of the country and the construction of a Socialist society, was the only correct one. He armed the Party and the working class with an indomitable faith in the victory of Socialist construction.

The Bolshevik Party, mustering its forces and resources, and brushing aside all capitulators and sceptics, led the country into a new historical phase —the phase of Socialist industrialization.

In this fight against the sceptics and capitulators, the Trotskyites, Zinovievites, Bukharins and Kamenevs, there was definitely welded together, after Lenin's incapacitation, that leading core of the Party —consisting of Stalin, Molotov, Kalinin, Voroshilov, Kuibyshev, Frunze, Dzerzhinsky, Kaganovich, Orjonikidze, Kirov, Yaroslavsky, Mikoyan, Andreyev,

J. V. Stalin and S. M. Kirov. Leningrad 1926
Photo

Shvernik, Zhdanov, Shkiryatov and others—that upheld the great banner of Lenin, rallied the Party behind Lenin's behests, and brought the Soviet people onto the broad road of industrialization and collective agriculture. The leader of this core and the guiding force of the Party and the state was Comrade Stalin.

Although he performed his task of leader of the Party and the people with consummate skill and enjoyed the unreserved support of the entire Soviet people, Stalin never allowed his work to be marred by the slightest hint of vanity, conceit or self-adulation. When interviewed by the German writer, Emil Ludwig, Stalin paid glowing tribute to Lenin's genius in transforming Russia, but of himself he simply said: "As for myself, I am merely a pupil of Lenin, and my aim is to be a worthy pupil of his."*

* J. V. Stalin, *Interview With the German Writer, Emil Ludwig.* Russ. ed., 1938, p. 3.

★

VIII

TO INDUSTRIALIZE in so brief a period of history a country so vast and at the same time so economically backward as was the Soviet Union at that time, was a task of tremendous difficulty. It was necessary to build up a large number of new industries, industries that had been unknown in tsarist Russia. It was necessary to create a defence industry, non-existent in old Russia. It was necessary to build plants for the production of modern agricultural machinery, such as the old countryside had never heard of. All this demanded enormous funds. In capitalist countries such funds were obtained by the merciless exploitation of the people, by wars of aggrandizement, by the bloodthirsty plunder of colonies and dependent countries, and by foreign loans. But the Soviet Union could not resort to such infamous means; and as to foreign loans, the capitalists had closed this source to the Soviet Union. The only way was to find these funds at home.

Guided by Lenin's precepts, Stalin developed the *doctrine of the Socialist industrialization* of the Soviet Union. He showed that:

1) Industrialization meant not merely increasing industrial output, but developing heavy industry, and above all its mainspring—machine building; for only a heavy industry, including a domestic machine-building industry, could provide the material basis for Socialism and render the Land of Socialism independent of the capitalist world;

2) The expropriation of the landlords and capitalists in our country as a result of the October Socialist Revolution, the abolition of the private ownership of the land, the factories, the banks, etc., and their conversion into common property of the people had created a mighty source of Socialist accumulation for the development of industry;

3) Socialist industrialization differs fundamentally from capitalist industrialization: the latter is based on the seizure and plunder of colonies, on military victories, on usurious loans, and on the merciless exploitation of the labouring masses and colonial peoples; Socialist industrialization is based on the social ownership of the means of production, on the accumulation and husbanding of the wealth created by the labour of the workers and peasants; it is necessarily accompanied by a steady rise in the standard of living of the labouring masses;

4) Hence the prime tasks in the struggle for industrialization were to raise productivity of labour, to reduce production costs, to promote labour discipline, strict economy, etc.;

5) The conditions for the building of Socialism existing in the U.S.S.R., and the labour enthusiasm of the working class, made it quite possible to achieve the necessary high speed of industrialization;

6) The reconstruction of agriculture on Socialist lines would have to be preceded by the industrialization of the country, so as to create the technical base for this reconstruction.

Armed with this clear and precise program, the working people of the Soviet Union embarked upon the Socialist industrialization of their country.

Alarmed by the progress of Socialist construction, the imperialists tried to frustrate, or at least to retard, the industrialization of the country by breaking off diplomatic and commercial relations with the U.S.S.R. (Britain), by assassinating Soviet ambassadors (Poland), by intensifying espionage and sabotage activities. At home, the Trotskyites, the Zinovievites, and the remnants of other, previously defeated, anti-Party groups joined in a treasonable bloc and launched a furious attack on the Party. "Something like a united front from Chamberlain to Trotsky is being formed," said Comrade Stalin at the time. Socialist industrialization could not be successful unless the Trotsky-Zinoviev bloc were routed ideologically and organizationally. And this was done by the Party, led by Comrade Stalin. Stalin's report on "The Social-Democratic Deviation in Our Party," at the Fifteenth Party Conference (November 1926), and his speech, "Once Again on the Social-Democratic Deviation in Our Party," at the Seventh Enlarged Plenum of the E.C.C.I. (December 1926), furnished the C.P.S.U.(B.) and the Communist International with the necessary ideological weapons, and ensured the solidarity and unity of the Party ranks.

The Enlarged Plenum of the E.C.C.I. stigmatized the adherents of the Trotsky-Zinoviev bloc as splitters who had sunk to downright Menshevism.

Having defeated and swept aside the capitulators and defenders of capitalism, the Bolsheviks carried on with the Socialist industrialization of the country.

There was not a single sphere or aspect of industrialization that escaped Stalin's attention. It was on his initiative that new industries were built and formerly backward industries reconstructed and expanded. It was he that inspired the creation of a second coal and metallurgical centre in our country —the Kuzbas. It was he that organized and directed the numerous Socialist construction projects. The Stalingrad Tractor Works, the Dnieper Power Station, the Magnitogorsk Iron and Steel Works, the Urals Engineering Works, the Rostov Agricultural Machinery Works, the Kuznetsk Coal and Iron Works, the Turkestan-Siberian Railway, the Saratov Harvester Combine Works, the automobile factories in Moscow and Gorky—all these and other industrial plants owed their initiation to Stalin.

The majestic and imposing edifice of Socialism that was being built in the U.S.S.R. exercised an irresistible influence on the workers of the capitalist countries. The U.S.S.R. became a veritable Mecca. Scores and hundreds of workers' delegations flocked to the Land of Soviets, and it was with keen interest and profound emotion that they saw how the workers, having ousted their exploiters, were building a new, Socialist society. They were interested in everything and wanted to know everything. On November 5, 1927, Stalin gave a long interview to workers' delegations from Germany, France, Austria, Czechoslovakia, China, Belgium and other countries.

By the end of 1927 the decisive success of the policy of Socialist industrialization was already unmistakable. The first results were summed up by the Fifteenth Party Congress, which met in December 1927. In his report on behalf of the Central Committee, Stalin drew a vivid picture of the progress of Socialist industrialization and emphasized the need for further extending and consolidating the Socialist key positions both in town and country, and for steering a course towards the complete elimination of capitalist elements from the national economy.

At the Congress, Stalin pointed out that agriculture was lagging behind industry, and indicated the way out of this situation which was jeopardizing the national economy as a whole.

"The way out," he said, "is to turn the small and scattered peasant farms into large united farms based on the common cultivation of the soil, to introduce collective cultivation of the soil on the basis of a new and higher technique.

"The way out is to unite the small and dwarf peasant farms gradually but surely, not by pressure, but by example and persuasion, into large farms based on common, cooperative, collective cultivation of the soil with the use of agricultural machines and tractors and scientific methods of intensive agriculture.

"There are no other ways."*

Why did the Soviet Union adopt the course of building up collective farming?

By the time of the Fifteenth Party Congress the retarded state of agriculture, particularly of grain farming, was becoming more and more marked. The gross grain harvest was approaching the prewar level, but the share of it actually available for the market, the amount of grain sold for the supply of the towns and the armed forces, was little more than one-third (thirty-seven per cent) of prewar. There were about twenty-five million small and dwarf peasant farms in the country. And small peasant farming was by its very nature a semi-natural form of economy, capable of supplying only a small quantity of

---

* J. V. Stalin, *Collected Works,* Russ. ed., Vol. 10, pp. 305-06.

grain for the market and incapable of extending production, of employing tractors and machinery, or of increasing harvest yields. The breaking up of the peasant farms was continuing, and the share of the grain harvest available for the market was declining.

"There could be no doubt that if such a state of affairs in grain farming were to continue, the army and the urban population would be faced with chronic famine."*

There were two possible ways of reconstructing the country's agriculture and creating large farms capable of employing tractors and agricultural machinery and of substantially increasing the marketable surplus of grain. One was to adopt large-scale *capitalist* farming, which would have meant the ruination of the peasant masses, created mass unemployment in the cities, destroyed the alliance between the working class and the peasantry, increased the strength of the kulaks, and led to the defeat of Socialism. And it was to this disastrous course that the Right capitulators and traitors were doing their utmost to commit the Party.

The other way was to take the course of amalgamating the small peasant holdings into large *socialist* farms, into collective farms, which would be able to use tractors and other modern machinery

---

* *History of the C.P.S.U.(B.), Short Course*, Moscow 1950, p. 353.

on an extensive scale for a rapid advancement of grain farming and a rapid increase in the marketable surplus of grain.

It is clear that the Bolshevik Party and the Soviet State could only take the second way, the *collective-farm* way of developing agriculture.

The Bolshevik Party was guided by Lenin's wise precept regarding the necessity of passing from small peasant farming to large-scale, collective, mechanized farming, which was alone capable of extricating the tens of millions of peasant farms from their age-old poverty.

"There is no escape from poverty for the small farm,"* Lenin had said.

The vital economic interests of the country, the needs of the people, demanded the adoption of collectivization. And the Bolshevik Party, led by Stalin, fully realized this vital economic need and was able to swing the peasant millions into the path of collectivization.

The Fifteenth Congress passed a resolution calling for the fullest development of collective farming. The Congress also gave instructions for the drawing up of the First Five-Year Plan for the development of the national economy. Thus, in the very midst of the work of Socialist industrialization,

* V. I. Lenin, *Collected Works*, 3rd Russ, ed., Vol. XXIV, p. 540.

Stalin outlined another immense task, the collectivization of agriculture. The accomplishment of this historic task entailed the most careful preparation, which for its profundity and scope may safely be compared to the preparations made for the Great October Socialist Revolution. The strategical genius of the proletarian revolution, boldly and unswervingly, yet cautiously and circumspectly, led the Party forward, breaking down all obstacles in the way to the envisaged goal, keeping a vigilant eye on the manoeuvres of the class enemy and unerringly foreseeing his next actions, regrouping the forces with a masterly hand in the very course of the offensive, consolidating the positions captured and utilizing the reserves to further the advance.

The Party created all the necessary material requisites for a mass influx of the peasantry into the collective farms. An industry was built up to supply the countryside with machines and tractors, for the technical re-equipment of agriculture. Sufficient funds were accumulated to finance the development of collective and state farming; some of the finest members of the Party and the working class were assigned to this work; already existing collective farms were consolidated to serve as examples of collective farming to the individual peasants. Machine and tractor stations and state farms were set up which helped the peasants to improve their methods of farming.

Realizing that their doom was imminent, the kulaks tried to resist. They organized a "grain strike," thinking to compel the Party, if not to capitulate, at least to retreat. In the same year, 1928, a big conspiratorial organization of wreckers, consisting of bourgeois experts, was discovered in the Shakhty District of the Donbas; similar organizations were later discovered in other districts. The wreckers had connections with imperialist states.

Led by Stalin, the Party adopted emergency measures against the kulaks and smashed their resistance. The wreckers were severely punished. Comrade Stalin called upon the Party to draw the necessary lessons from the Shakhty affair, and demanded that Bolshevik business executives must themselves become experts in the technique of production and that the training of new technicians drawn from the ranks of the working class must be accelerated.

In 1928-29, when the Party launched the offensive against the kulaks, Bukharin, Rykov, Tomsky, and their whole anti-Party gang of Right capitulators and would-be restorers of capitalism, rose up to replace the Trotskyites and Zinovievites who had been smashed by the Party. At the same time the imperialists, relying on the capitulatory activities of the Rights, made a new attempt to involve the U.S.S.R. in war. The British and French General Staffs drew up plans for another attempt at military intervention in the U.S.S.R., to take place in 1929 or 1930.

Just as the victory of the Great Socialist Revolution in October 1917 would have been impossible if the capitulators and scabs, the Mensheviks and the S.R.'s, had not been put to rout, so the victory of Socialism in the countryside would have been impossible if the Right capitulators had not been routed in 1928-29. A cardinal factor in the victory of the Party over the Bukharin-Rykov anti-Party group were Stalin's speeches on "The Right Danger in the C.P.S.U.(B.)" at the Plenum of the Moscow Committee and the Moscow Control Commission of the Party in October 1928, and on "The Right Deviation in the C.P.S.U.(B.)" at the Plenum of the Central Committee of the Party in April 1929.

In these speeches Stalin utterly exposed the Rights as enemies of Leninism, and showed that they were agents of the kulaks in the Party.

In the fight against the Rights Stalin cemented the Party and led it in the assault against the last stronghold of capitalist exploitation in our country. Stalin's genius, his inflexible will and sagacious insight advanced the revolution to a new and higher stage. In "A Year of Great Change," the historic article he wrote in 1929 on the occasion of the twelfth anniversary of the October Revolution, he said:

"The past year witnessed a great *change* on all fronts of Socialist construction. The change expressed itself, and is still expressing itself, in a determined *offensive* of Socialism against the capitalist elements in town and country. The characteristic feature of this offensive is that it has already brought us a number of decisive *successes* in the principal spheres of the Socialist reconstruction of our national economy"*

The Party succeeded in bringing about a radical change in the sphere of productivity of labour. One of the most difficult problems of Socialist industrialization—the problem of accumulating financial resources for the development of heavy industry—was in the main solved. The Party succeeded in bringing about a radical change in the development of our agriculture and of our peasantry. The collective-farm movement began to advance by leaps and bounds, even surpassing large-scale industry in rate of development. It was becoming a mass movement.

"The new and decisive feature of the present collective-farm movement," Stalin wrote, "is that the peasants are joining the collective farms not in separate groups, as was formerly the case, but in whole villages, whole volosts, whole districts, and even whole areas. And what does that mean? It means that *the middle peasant has joined the collective-farm movement*. And that is the basis of that radical change in the development of agriculture which represents the most important achievement of the Soviet government...."**

* J. V. Stalin, *Collected Works*, Russ. ed., Vol. 12, p. 118.
** *Ibid.*, p. 132.

Thus, under Stalin's guidance, the way was paved for the historic transition from the policy of restricting and squeezing out the kulak elements to the policy of eliminating the kulaks as a class, on the basis of solid collectivization.

This was a period when industrialization and collectivization were only gathering momentum, and when it was necessary to muster the labour forces of the people to the utmost for the accomplishment of tasks of the greatest magnitude. And it was a paramount service that Stalin rendered in choosing this moment to bring prominently to the fore the question of the status of woman, of woman's work, of her all-important role in society and her contribution to the labour effort as a worker or peasant, and in stressing the important role she had to play in economic, public and social life. Having given the problem of woman the salience it deserved, Stalin indicated the only correct lines along which it could be solved.

"There has not been a single great movement of the oppressed in history in which working women have not played a part. Working women, who are the most oppressed of all the oppressed, have never stood aloof, and could not stand aloof, from the great march of emancipation. We know that the movement for the emancipation of the slaves had its hundreds and thousands of women martyrs and heroines. Tens of thousands of working women took their

J. V. Stalin on deck of the cruiser *Chervona Ukraina*, of the Black Sea Fleet. July 25, 1929

Photo

place in the ranks of the fighters for the emancipation of the serfs. And it is not surprising that the revolutionary movement of the working class, the most powerful of all the emancipatory movements of the oppressed masses, has attracted millions of working women to its standard."*

"The working women," Stalin further said, "the women industrial workers and peasants, constitute one of the biggest reserves of the working class, a reserve that represents a good half of the population. Whether this women's reserve goes with the working class or against it will determine the fate of the proletarian movement, the victory or defeat of the proletarian revolution, the victory or defeat of the proletarian government. The first task, therefore, of the proletariat and of its vanguard, the Communist Party, is to wage a resolute struggle to wrest women, the women workers and peasants, from the influence of the bourgeoisie, to politically educate and to organize the women workers and peasants under the banner of the proletariat."**

"But working women," Stalin went on to say, "are something more than a reserve. They may become and should become—if the working class pursues a correct policy—a regular army of the work-

* J. V. Stalin, *Collected Works*, Russ. ed., Vol. 7, p. 48
** *Ibid*, pp. 48-49.

ing class operating against the bourgeoisie. To mould the women's labour reserve into an army of women workers and peasants fighting shoulder to shoulder with the great army of the proletariat—that is the second and decisive task of the working class."*

As for the role and significance of women in the collective farms, Stalin expressed his views on this subject at the First Congress of Collective-Farm Shock Workers. He said:

"The woman question in the collective farms is a big question, comrades. I know that many of you underrate the women and even laugh at them. That is a mistake, comrades, a serious mistake. The point is not only that women comprise half the population. Primarily, the point is that the collective-farm movement has advanced a number of remarkable and capable women to leading positions. Look at this Congress, at the delegates, and you will realize that women have long since advanced from the ranks of the backward to the ranks of the forward. The women in the collective farms are a great force. To keep this force down would be criminal. It is our duty to bring the women in the collective farms forward and to make use of this great force."**

---

* J. V. Stalin, *Collected Works*, Russ. ed., Vol. 7, p. 49.
** J. V. Stalin, *Problems of Leninism*, Moscow 1947, p. 450.

"As for the women collective farmers themselves," Stalin went on, "they must remember the power and significance of the collective farms for women; they must remember that only in the collective farm do they have the opportunity of becoming equal with men. Without collective farms—inequality; in collective farms—equal rights. Let our comrades, the women collective farmers, remember this and let them cherish the collective-farm system as the apple of their eye."*

The enlistment in the work of building Socialism of the broad masses of our country, including the working people of the formerly oppressed and backward nations, was a signal triumph for the Soviet ideology, which regards the masses as the real makers of history, over the bourgeois ideology, which insistently inculcates the absurd idea that the masses are incapable of independent creative endeavour in any sphere of life. Stalin exposed the reactionary essence of the "theory" that the exploited cannot get along without the exploiters. "One of the most important results of the October Revolution is that it dealt this false 'theory' a mortal blow," Stalin said.**

Stalin likewise exposed the reactionary legend that nations are divided into superior and inferior races.

* *Ibid.*, pp. 450-51.
** J. V. Stalin, *Collected Works*, Russ. ed., Vol. 10, p. 242.

"It was formerly the 'accepted idea' that the world has been divided from time immemorial into inferior and superior races, into blacks and whites, of whom the former are unfit for civilization and are doomed to be objects of exploitation, while the latter are the only vehicles of civilization, whose mission it is to exploit the former.

"This legend must now be regarded as shattered and discarded. One of the most important results of the October Revolution is that it dealt this legend a mortal blow, having demonstrated in practice that liberated non-European nations, drawn into the channel of Soviet development, are not a bit less capable of promoting a *really* progressive culture and a *really* progressive civilization than are the European nations."*

* J. V. Stalin, *Collected Works*, Russ. ed., Vol. 10, pp. 243-44.

★

IX

ON DECEMBER 27, 1929, Stalin addressed a conference of Marxist students of the agrarian question. He exposed the bourgeois theory of "equilibrium" of the various sectors of the national economy, and demolished the anti-Marxist theories of "spontaneity" in Socialist construction and of the "stability" of small peasant farming. Having disposed of these bourgeois, anti-Marxist, Right-opportunist theories, he proceeded to make a profound analysis of the nature of collective farming as a Socialist form of economy, and demonstrated the necessity for a transition to the policy of solid collectivization of agriculture, and, on this basis, to the elimination of the kulaks as a class.

At the Eleventh Party Congress Lenin had spoken of the last, decisive fight against Russian capitalism, to which small peasant economy gives rise. But at that time it was impossible to say exactly when that fight would take place. Now Comrade Stalin, with his insight of genius, scientifically proved that the *moment* of the last, decisive fight against domestic capitalism had already arrived. A master of dialectics, he showed that the elimination of the kulaks as a class was not a continuation of the former policy of restricting and squeezing out the kulaks, but a sharp *turn* in the policy of the Party.

"While the confiscation of the landed estates was the *first* step of the October Revolution in the country-side," it was stated in the resolution of the Six-teenth Party Congress, "the adoption of collective farming is the *second*, and, moreover, a decisive, step, marking a most important stage in the process of laying the foundations of Socialist society in the U.S.S.R."*

The peasantry came to adopt a Socialist form of husbandry because economic necessity demanded a change to large-scale cooperative farming, to collective, mechanized agriculture. For a number of years the Bolshevik Party and the Soviet State had been fostering new productive forces in the countryside, introducing modern machinery—tractors, harvester combines, etc.—and training skilled forces for Socialist farming, millions of people who were mastering modern technique.

In his historic message congratulating the workers of the Stalingrad Tractor Works on its opening day (June 17, 1930), Stalin wrote:

---

* *C.P.S.U.(B.): Resolutions and Decisions of Congresses, Conferences and Plenary Sessions of the Central Committee,* Part II, 6th Russ. ed., 1941, p. 428.

"Greetings and congratulations to the workers and executives of the giant Red Banner Tractor Plant, the first in the U.S.S.R., on their victory. The 50,000 tractors which you are to produce for our country every year will be 50,000 projectiles shattering the old, bourgeois world and clearing the way for the new, Socialist system in the countryside. My best wishes for the fulfilment of your program."*

The new productive forces which had been created in the countryside inevitably gave rise to new, *Socialist* relations between man and man.

Concretely elaborating the Marxist-Leninist theory of Socialism from every aspect, Stalin demonstrated that the transition to collectivization could not be in the form of a simple and peaceful influx of the peasants into the collective farms, but would entail a struggle of the peasant masses against the kulaks. The kulaks would have to be defeated in open battle in full view of the peasantry, so that the peasants might see for themselves how weak the capitalist elements were. Hence solid collectivization was organically linked with the elimination of the kulaks as a class.

Comrade Stalin's indication of the necessity for a turn in Party policy from restricting the exploiting proclivities of the kulaks to eliminating the kulaks

* J. V. Stalin, *Collected Works*, Russ. ed., Vol. 12, p. 234.

as a class formed the basis of the resolution on "The Rate of Collectivization and State Measures to Assist the Development of Collective Farms," adopted by the Central Committee on January 5, 1930.

The enemies of the Party did their utmost to frustrate the Party's policy of collectivizing agriculture. These hostile attempts found expression, not only in open attacks on collectivization by the Right capitulators, but also in "Leftist" distortions of the Party line, in violations of the pace of collectivization laid down by the Party and of the Leninist-Stalinist principle that the formation of collective farms must be voluntary, in pigheaded attempts to skip the artel form and pass straight to the commune, and in compulsory socialization of dwellings, small livestock, poultry, and the like.

The enemies at home and abroad, the interventionists and their agents, hoped that these "Leftist," and sometimes deliberately provocative, practices, would incense the peasantry against the Soviet regime. The General Staffs of the imperialist powers were already fixing the date for an attempt at another intervention. But the leader of the Party saw the new danger in time.

On March 2, 1930, by decision of the Central Committee, Stalin published his article, "Dizzy With Success," in which he rebuffed the "Leftist" distortions of policy as jeopardizing the collective-farm movement. "The article laid the utmost emphasis on the principle that the formation of collective farms must be voluntary, and on the necessity of making allowances for the diversity of conditions in the various districts of the U.S.S.R. when determining the pace and methods of collectivization. Comrade Stalin reiterated that the chief form of the collective-farm movement was the agricultural artel. ... Comrade Stalin's article was of the utmost political moment. It helped the Party organizations to rectify their mistakes and dealt a severe blow to the enemies of the Soviet power who had been hoping to take advantage of the distortions of policy to set the peasants against the Soviet power."*

While dealing a crushing blow to the "Leftist" distortions, and at the same time shattering the hopes of the interventionists, Comrade Stalin, as the teacher of the masses, explained to the Party and non-Party cadres wherein lies the art of leadership.

"The art of leadership," he wrote, "is a serious matter. One must not lag behind the movement, because to do so is to lose contact with the masses. But neither must one rush ahead, because to rush ahead is to lose the masses and isolate oneself. He who wants to lead a movement and at the same time keep in touch with the vast masses must wage

---

* *History of the C.P.S.U.(B.), Short Course*, Moscow 1950, p. 380.

a fight on two fronts—against those who lag behind and against those who rush on ahead."*

On April 3, 1930, Stalin followed this up with another article, his "Reply to Collective Farm Comrades," addressed to the collective farm millions, in which he exposed the root cause of the mistakes in the peasant question and the major blunders committed in the collective-farm movement, and, with irresistible logic, explained the essential laws of an offensive on the class war front. It is impossible to conduct an offensive, he pointed out, without consolidating positions already captured, without regrouping forces, without supplying the front with reserves, and without bringing up the rear services. The opportunists did not understand the class nature of the offensive: against which class, and in alliance with which class, it was being conducted. It was not any kind of offensive we needed, Stalin wrote, but an offensive in alliance with the middle peasants against the kulaks.

Thanks to Stalin's guidance, the distortions were rectified and a firm basis was created for a further mighty advance in the collective-farm movement. Headed by Comrade Stalin, the Party solved what was, after the conquest of power, the most difficult problem of the proletarian revolution, the problem

* J. V. Stalin, *Collected Works*, Russ. ed., Vol. 12, p. 199.

of placing the small peasant farms on Socialist lines and of eliminating the kulaks, the largest of the exploiting classes.

"This was a profound revolution, a leap from an old qualitative state of society to a new qualitative state, equivalent in its consequences to the revolution of October 1917.

"The distinguishing feature of this revolution is that it was accomplished *from above*, on the initiative of the state, and directly supported *from below* by the millions of peasants, who were fighting to throw off kulak bondage and to live in freedom in the collective farms."*

Guided by Lenin's pronouncements on the necessity of passing from small peasant farming to large-scale, cooperative, collective farming, and taking Lenin's cooperative plan as a basis, Stalin worked out and gave practical effect to *the theory of the collectivization of agriculture*. His new contributions to this sphere were the following:

1) He comprehensively elaborated the problem of collective farming as a form of Socialist rural economy;

2) He showed that the key link in collective-farm development at the present stage is the agricultural artel, for it is the most rational and the most

---

* *History of the C.P.S.U.(B), Short Course*, Moscow 1950, p. 376.

comprehensible to the peasants, making it possible to combine the personal interests of the collective farmers with their collective interests, to adapt their personal interests to the public interests;

3) He showed that the policy of restricting and squeezing out the kulaks must be changed to one of eliminating them as a class, on the basis of solid collectivization;

4) He revealed the significance of the machine and tractor stations as points of support in the Socialist reorganization of agriculture and as a means by which the Socialist State rendered assistance to agriculture and the peasantry.

In February 1930, in response to numerous requests from organizations and from general meetings of workers, peasants and Red Army men, the Central Executive Committee of the U.S.S.R. conferred upon Stalin a second Order of the Red Banner, for his outstanding services in the construction of Socialism.

The Sixteenth Party Congress, which sat from June 26 to July 13, 1930, has gone down in history as the Congress of the sweeping offensive of Socialism along the whole front. In his report, Stalin explained the significance of this sweeping offensive of Socialism against the capitalist elements along the whole front, and showed that the Soviet Union *had already entered the period of Socialism.*

Reporting to the Congress on the results achieved in the work of industrializing the country and collectivizing agriculture, he went on to outline the new tasks that confronted us in the new period of development. While we had overtaken and outstripped the advanced capitalist countries in *rate* of development, we were still far behind them as regards the *level* of industrial output. Hence the need for a further acceleration of the speed of development in order to overtake and outstrip the capitalist countries in level of industrial output as well. Comrade Stalin then proceeded to explain what the Party must do in order to ensure the fulfilment of the First Five-Year Plan in four years.

The working people of the whole country applied themselves enthusiastically to the accomplishment of the gigantic tasks set by the Congress. Socialist emulation and shock work developed on a wide scale. By the time of the Sixteenth Congress no less than two million workers were taking part in the Socialist emulation movement, while over a million workers belonged to shock brigades.

"The most remarkable feature of emulation," Comrade Stalin said at the Sixteenth Congress, "is the radical revolution it brings with it in men's views of labour, for it transforms labour from a degrading and painful burden, as it was regarded before, into a matter of *honour*, a matter of *glory*, a matter of *valour* and *heroism*. There is not, nor can there be, anything similar to it in capitalist countries."[*]

The fulfilment of the First Five-Year Plan called for the reconstruction of every branch of the national economy on the basis of new and up-to-date technique. Technique was becoming a matter of decisive importance. In this connection, the leader of the Party, in his speech on "The Tasks of Business Executives" at the First All-Union Conference of Managers of Socialist Industry, on February 4, 1931, put forward a new slogan: "Bolsheviks must master technique"; "In the period of reconstruction technique decides everything."

At a time when the Party was engaged in the strenuous work of building Socialism, it became increasingly important to educate the members and candidate members of the Party in the teachings of Marxism-Leninism, to study the historical experience of the Bolshevik Party, and to wage a fight against all falsifiers of the history of the Party.

In November 1931 Stalin published his well-known letter to the magazine *Proletarskaya Revolutsia.* Its effect in consolidating the ideological unity of the Party has been immense. In this letter Stalin denounced the Trotskyite falsifiers of the history of

---

[*] J. V. Stalin, *Collected Works*, Russ. ed., Vol. 12, p. 315.

Bolshevism, and pointed out that Leninism had originated, matured and grown strong in a relentless struggle against opportunism of all brands, that the Bolsheviks were the only revolutionary organization in the world to have utterly routed the opportunists and centrists and driven them from its ranks. He forcefully showed that Trotskyism is the vanguard of the counter-revolutionary bourgeoisie, a force fighting Communism, the Soviet system, and the construction of Socialism in the U.S.S.R.

The First Five-Year Plan was fulfilled by the beginning of 1933—ahead of schedule. At a plenary meeting of the Central Committee and the Central Control Commission of the Party, held in January 1933, Stalin reported on "The Results of the First Five-Year Plan." Our country, he said, had been transformed from an agrarian into an industrial country, from a country of small peasants into a country with an advanced, Socialist agriculture, conducted on the largest scale in the world. The exploiting classes had been dislodged from their positions in production. The remnants of them had scattered over the face of the country and were carrying on the fight against the Soviet regime by stealth. It was therefore essential to heighten vigilance, to wage a fight for the protection of Socialist property—the foundation of the Soviet system— and to strengthen the dictatorship of the proletariat to the utmost.

In another speech at this plenary meeting of the Central Committee and Central Control Commission—on "Work in the Rural Districts"—Stalin made a profound analysis of the defects in Party work in the countryside and outlined an exhaustive program of measures for the consolidation of the collective-farm system.

A new task now faced the Party. The fight now was to consolidate the collective farms, to organize work in the collective farms on proper lines, to make them Bolshevik collective farms, and to purge them of hostile kulak elements and wreckers. For this purpose Comrade Stalin proposed that political departments be set up in the machine and tractor stations and the state farms. In the space of two years (1933-34) the political departments of the machine and tractor stations did a great deal to consolidate the collective farms.

At the First All-Union Congress of Collective-Farm Shock Workers, held on February 19, 1933, Comrade Stalin proclaimed the slogan: "Make the collective farms Bolshevik and the collective farmers prosperous," and showed how this was to be accomplished.

"Only one thing is now needed for the collective farmers to become prosperous," Stalin said, "and that is for them to work in the collective farms conscientiously; to make efficient use of the tractors and machines; to make efficient use of the draught cattle; to cultivate the land efficiently and to cherish collective-farm property."*

Stalin's speech impressed itself on the minds of the millions of collective farmers and became a practical program of action for the collective farms.

In his review of the experience of Socialist construction, Comrade Stalin took up the question of Soviet trade and showed that it was the form of distribution and exchange of the products of labour under Socialism. He said:

"Soviet trade is trade without capitalists, big or small; it is trade without profiteers, big or small. It is a special form of trade, which has never existed in history before, and which is practised only by us, the Bolsheviks, under the conditions of Soviet development."**

"If the economic life of the country is to make rapid progress, and industry and agriculture to have a stimulus for further increasing their output," he said on another occasion, "one more condition is necessary—namely, fully developed *trade* between town and country, between the various districts and regions of the country, between the various branches of the national economy."***

---

* J. V. Stalin, *Problems of Leninism*, Moscow 1947, p. 448.
** *Ibid.*, p. 419.
*** *Ibid.*, p. 493.

He sharply criticized those who underrated the importance of Soviet trade or treated it with scorn. "There is still among a section of Communists," he said, "a supercilious, contemptuous attitude towards trade in general, and towards Soviet trade in particular. These Communists, save the mark, look upon Soviet trade as a thing of secondary importance, hardly worth bothering about, and regard those engaged in trade as doomed.... These people do not realize that Soviet trade is our own, Bolshevik, work, and that the workers employed in trade, including those behind the counter—if only they work conscientiously—are doing our revolutionary, Bolshevik, work."*

These utterances of Comrade Stalin on the subject of trade were of great importance in expanding commodity exchange in the country and strengthening Soviet trade.

Speaking on the activities of the Central Committee of the C.P.S.U.(B.) in Leningrad on the eve of the Seventeenth Congress of the Party, Sergei Kirov, that inspired tribune of the revolution and a man the Party loved, paid the following tribute to the great organizer of the Socialist victories of the working class:

"Comrades, when one speaks of the services of our Party, of its achievements, one cannot help

---

* J. V. Stalin, *Problems of Leninism*, Moscow 1947, pp. 493-94.

speaking of *the great organizer of the gigantic victories we have achieved. I refer to Comrade Stalin.*

"I must say that he is a truly accomplished, a truly perfect successor and continuer of the cause committed to our care by the great founder of our Party, whom we lost ten years ago.

"It is not easy to grasp the figure of Stalin in all its gigantic proportions. *In these latter years, ever since we have had to carry on our work without Lenin, there has been no major development in our labours, no new undertaking, slogan or trend of policy of any importance of which Comrade Stalin was not the author. All the principal work—and this the Party should know—is done in accordance with the instructions, on the initiative, and under the guidance of Comrade Stalin.* The decisions on the most important problems of international policy are made according to his recommendations. And not only important problems, but even what might seem third-rate, even tenth-rate problems interest him, if they affect the workers, the peasants, the labouring people generally of our country.

"I must say that this applies not only to the construction of Socialism as a whole, but to the various aspects of our work as well. For instance, if we take the defence of our country, it must be emphatically stressed that it is entirely to Stalin that we are indebted for all the achievements which I have mentioned.

"The mighty will and organizational genius of this man ensure our Party the timely accomplishment of the big historical turns involved in the victorious construction of Socialism.

"Take Comrade Stalin's slogans—'Make the collective farmer prosperous,' 'Make the collective farms Bolshevik,' 'Master technique' and his six historic conditions—all that goes to direct the construction of Socialism at the present stage of our work emanates from this man, and all that we have achieved in the period of the First Five-Year Plan has been due to his directions."*

Comrade Stalin guided the labours of the Seventeenth Congress of the Party, which met at the beginning of 1934, and which is known as the *Congress of Victors*. In his report to this Congress on the work of the Central Committee, he reviewed the historic victories of the Party, the victories of Socialism in the U.S.S.R.

He spoke of the triumph of the policy of industrialization, and of the policy of the solid collectivization of agriculture and the elimination of the kulaks as a class; he spoke of the triumph of the doctrine that Socialism could be built in one country. The Socialist formation, he showed, now held undivided sway over the entire national econ-

---

* S. M. Kirov, *Selected Speeches and Articles, 1912-34,* Russ. ed., Moscow 1939, pp. 609-10.

omy, while all the other social-economic formations had gone to the bottom. The collective-farm system had triumphed finally and completely.

But Stalin warned the Party that the fight was by no means over. Although the enemies had been smashed, survivals of their ideology still lingered and often made their influence felt. The U.S.S.R. was still encircled by a capitalist world, which kept alive the survivals of capitalism in the minds of people and utilized them for its own ends.

The survivals of capitalism in the minds of men, Comrade Stalin pointed out, were much more tenacious in the sphere of the national question than in any other. In reply to the question—which deviation in the national question was the major danger: the deviation towards Great-Russian nationalism or the deviation towards local nationalism?— Comrade Stalin said that under present conditions "the major danger is the deviation against which we have ceased to fight, thereby allowing it to grow into a danger to the state."*

Hence the need for systematic effort to overcome the survivals of capitalism in the minds of men, for systematic criticism of the ideologies of all trends hostile to Leninism, for the tireless propaganda of Leninism, for raising the ideological level of the

* J. V. Stalin, *Problems of Leninism*, Moscow 1947, p. 507.

Party members, and for the internationalist education of the working people. Stalin laid special stress on the need for greater vigilance on the part of the Party:

"We must not lull the Party," he said, "but sharpen its vigilance; we must not lull it to sleep, but keep it ready for action; not disarm it, but arm it; not demobilize it, but hold it in a state of mobilization for the fulfilment of the Second Five-Year Plan."*

Stalin in this report outlined a concrete program for the future work of the Party in the sphere of industry, agriculture, trade and transport. He also outlined a program of organizational measures (training of personnel, checking up on fulfilment, etc.). The task, he said, was "to raise organizational leadership to the level of political leadership." He further mapped a program in the sphere of culture, science, education and the ideological struggle.

Comrade Stalin also dwelt in this report on the foreign policy of the U.S.S.R. An economic crisis was rampant in the capitalist world, he said, and feverish preparations for war were being made in a number of countries, especially in Germany, since the fascists had come to power. Amid these economic upheavals and military and political cataclysms,

* J. V. Stalin, *Problems of Leninism*, Moscow 1947, p. 517.

J. V. Stalin and A. M. Gorky
Photo

the U.S.S.R. held firmly and unwaveringly to its course of peace, fighting the danger of war and persistently pursuing a policy of peace.

"Our foreign policy is clear," Comrade Stalin said. "It is a policy of preserving peace and strengthening commercial relations with all countries. The U.S.S.R. does not think of threatening anybody—let alone of attacking anybody. We stand for peace and champion the cause of peace. But we are not afraid of threats and are prepared to answer the instigators of war blow for blow.... Those who try to attack our country will receive a crushing repulse to teach them not to poke their pig snouts into our Soviet garden."*

On the motion of Sergei Kirov, the Seventeenth Congress endorsed Comrade Stalin's report in toto as a Congress decision, as a Party law, as the Party's program of work for the coming period. The Congress also endorsed the Second Five-Year Plan for the development of the national economy.

---

* *Ibid.*, p. 469.

★

X

THE SUCCESS of the general line of the Party was expressed in a continued and steady progress of the country's industry and agriculture. In the sphere of industry, the Second Stalin Five-Year Plan was fulfilled by April 1937, ahead of schedule—in four years and three months. With the completion of the reconstruction of industry and agriculture, our national economy found itself equipped with the most advanced technique in the world. Our industry had received a vast quantity of machines, machine tools and other implements of production. Our agriculture had received first-class Soviet tractors, harvester combines and other complex agricultural machines. The transport system had received first-class motor vehicles, locomotives, ships and aeroplanes. The armed forces had received new, excellent equipment—artillery, tanks, aircraft and warships.

This titanic labour of technical re-equipment of our national economy was directly guided by Comrade Stalin. New makes of machines, important technical innovations or inventions were, and are, introduced under his direct instructions. He personally acquainted himself with all the details of the work of technical reconstruction of industry and agriculture, inspiring and enthusing workers and engineers, factory managers and economic administrators, inventors and designers. He directed particular attention and care to the technical equipment of the Red Army, Air Force and Navy, the result of which has been to make them the formidable force they are to the enemies of Socialism.

One of the major problems of Socialist construction the Party had to tackle was the training by Soviet society of its own cadres, the creation by the Soviet people and primarily by the working class of its own intelligentsia. This was one of the cardinal problems of Socialist construction. In the light of Lenin's view that Socialist revolution was the basic condition for the rapid cultural progress of the masses, Comrade Stalin regarded the development of the cultural forces of the working class as one of the decisive factors of Socialist construction. He said:

"Among the ruling classes that have hitherto existed, the working class, as a ruling class, occupies a rather unique and not altogether favourable position in history. All ruling classes till now—the slave-owners, the landowners, the capitalists—were also wealthy classes. They were able to educate their sons in the science and art of government. The working class differs from them, among other things, in that it is not a wealthy class, that it formerly was not able to educate its sons in the science and art of government, and has become able to do so only now, after it has come to power.

"That, incidentally, is the reason why the question of a cultural revolution is so acute with us."[*]

This problem of training skilled and expert forces from the workers' midst became very urgent when our country was already abundantly supplied with new machinery and an acute need was felt for people who had mastered the use of machinery, people capable of utilizing it to the full for the benefit of our Motherland.

This new machinery, this mighty technique, required trained people capable of harnessing it and extracting from it all that it could give. The attention of our cadres had to be sharply turned to the need for mastering this new technique, to the need for intensifying to the utmost the work of training large numbers of people capable of utilizing this technique with the maximum effect. And in this respect, Stalin's address to the graduates from the Red Army Academies in May 1935 was of exceptional importance:

"In order to set technique going," he said, "and to utilize it to the full, we need people who have mastered technique, we need cadres capable of mastering and utilizing this technique according to

[*] J. V. Stalin, *Collected Works*, Russ. ed., Vol. 11, pp. 37-38.

all the rules of the art. Without people who have mastered technique, technique is dead. In the charge of people who have mastered technique, technique can and should perform miracles. If in our first-class mills and factories, in our state farms and collective farms, in our transport system and in our Red Army we had sufficient cadres capable of harnessing this technique, our country would secure results three times and four times as great as at present.... It is time to realize that of all the valuable capital the world possesses, the most valuable and most decisive is people, cadres. It must be realized that under our present conditions 'cadres decide everything.' If we have good and numerous cadres in industry, agriculture, transport, and the army—our country will be invincible. If we do not have such cadres—we shall be lame on both legs."*

Comrade Stalin's speech served as a powerful stimulus to the solution of one of the cardinal problems of Socialist construction—the problem of cadres. The effect of this pronouncement by the leader of the Party was not only to direct the attention of all Party and Soviet organizations to the problem of cadres, it also awakened a wide response among the masses, and aroused in them a new labour enthusiasm.

* J. V. Stalin, *Problems of Leninism*, Moscow 1947, pp. 523-24.

Upon the initiative of advanced rank-and-file workers there arose the mighty *Stakhanov movement*. Originating in the coal industry of the Donbas, it spread with incredible speed to all parts of the country, and to all branches of the national economy. Tens and hundreds of thousands of splendid heroes of labour in industry, in the transport system and in agriculture, set an example in mastering technique and in Socialist productivity of labour.

Comrade Stalin explained to the Party and the whole country the epoch-making significance of this new movement. Speaking at the First All-Union Conference of Stakhanovites, in November 1935, he said that the Stakhanov movement "is the expression of a new wave of Socialist emulation, a new and higher stage of Socialist emulation.... The significance of the Stakhanov movement lies in the fact that it is a movement which is smashing the old technical standards, because they are inadequate, which in a number of cases is surpassing the productivity of labour of the foremost capitalist countries, and is thus creating the practical possibility of further consolidating Socialism in our country, the possibility of converting our country into the most prosperous of all countries."*

---

* J. V. Stalin, *Problems of Leninism*, Moscow 1947, pp. 526-27.

Comrade Stalin showed that the Stakhanov movement was paving the way to Communism, that it bore within it the seed of a cultural and technical advancement of the working class which would lead to the obliteration of the distinction between mental and manual labour.

Speaking of the conditions that had made the Stakhanov movement possible, Comrade Stalin showed wherein lies the might and invincibility of our revolution.

"Our revolution," he said, "is the only one which not only smashed the fetters of capitalism and brought the people freedom, but also succeeded in creating the material conditions of a prosperous life for the people. Therein lies the strength and invincibility of our revolution."*

Stalin personally guided the work of the All-Union Conference of Stakhanovites and of other conferences of foremost workers in industry, transport, and agriculture, held in the Kremlin. He discussed with Stakhanovites in industry and transport, with harvester combine operators, tractor drivers, dairymaids, heroines of the beet fields, the details of technique and organization of production in all branches of the national economy.

Together with members of the Party Central Committee and the Government he received in the

---

* *Ibid.*, p. 532.

Kremlin many delegations from the fraternal Social-ist Republics. This was a vivid demonstration of the great friendship binding the peoples of the Soviet Union—the fruit of the national policy of Lenin and Stalin. In conjunction with leading industrial work-ers and collective farmers, Comrade Stalin and his colleagues worked out many a momentous decision on some of the most important questions of Social-ist construction.

"Lenin taught us that only such leaders can be real Bolshevik leaders as know not only how to teach the workers and peasants but also how to learn from them," said Comrade Stalin at the conference of Stakhanovites. And, from the earliest days of his revolutionary career, he himself has always set an ideal example of such contact with the masses.

The Socialist reconstruction of the entire nation-al economy brought about a radical change in the correlation of classes in the country. This called for changes in the Constitution which had been adopted in 1924; and a proposal to this effect was made, on Comrade Stalin's initiative, by the Central Commit-tee of the Party at the Seventh Congress of Soviets of the U.S.S.R.

A Constitution Commission, under Comrade Stalin's chairmanship, prepared a draft of a new Constitution. This draft was thrown open for nation-wide discussion, which continued for five and a half months. There was not a corner in the country

J. V. Stalin surrounded by children at the
Tushino Aerodrome. 1936

Photo

where this greatest document in human history was not studied and discussed. The draft Constitution was received with great joy and pride by the whole Soviet people.

In his report at the Extraordinary Eighth Congress of Soviets on November 25, 1936, Comrade Stalin made a profound analysis of the draft of the new Constitution, bringing out the tremendous changes which had taken place in our country since the adoption of the Constitution of 1924. The victory of Socialism now made it possible to extend the democratic principles of the election system and to introduce universal, equal and direct suffrage with secret ballot.

All the gigantic victories of Socialism are embodied in the Constitution of the U.S.S.R. The Constitution states that Soviet society consists of two friendly classes—the workers and the peasants. The political foundation of the U.S.S.R. is the Soviets of Working People's Deputies. The economic foundation of the U.S.S.R. is the Socialist ownership of the means of production. All citizens of the U.S.S.R. are ensured the right to work, to rest and leisure, to education, to maintenance in old age or in case of illness or incapacitation. The equality of all citizens, irrespective of nationality, race or sex, is an indefeasible law. In the interests of the consolidation of Socialist society, the Constitution guarantees freedom of speech, freedom of the press, freedom of assembly, including the holding of mass meetings, the right to unite in public organizations, inviolability of the person, inviolability of homes and privacy of correspondence. The right of asylum is afforded to foreign citizens persecuted for defending the interests of the working people, or for their scientific activities, or for participation in the struggle for national emancipation. These great rights and liberties of the working people, unprecedented in history, are guaranteed materially and economically by the whole Socialist economic system, which knows no crises, anarchy or unemployment.

At the same time the Constitution of the U.S.S.R. imposes on all citizens serious obligations: to observe the laws, to maintain labour discipline, honestly to perform their public duties, to respect the rules of Socialist human intercourse, to cherish and safeguard Socialist property, and to defend the Socialist fatherland.

What the best and most progressive minds of humanity had dreamed of for hundreds of years has been made an indefeasible law by the Constitution of the U.S.S.R.—the Constitution of Socialism victorious and of fully developed, Socialist democracy.

The new Constitution was approved and adopted by the Eighth Extraordinary Congress of Soviets, on December 5, 1936. It is unanimously called by the peoples of the U.S.S.R. after its author—Stalin. For the working people of the U.S.S.R. the Stalin Constitution is a summary and seal of their struggles and achievements; for the working people of the capitalist countries it is a great program of struggle. It is the endorsement of the historic fact that the U.S.S.R. has entered a new phase of development, the phase of the completion of the building of Socialist society and the gradual transition to Communism. It is a moral and political weapon in the hands of the working people of the world in their struggle against bourgeois reaction. It shows that what has been accomplished in the U.S.S.R. can be accomplished in other countries too.

Stalin spoke of the international significance of the Constitution of the U.S.S.R.:

"Today, when the turbid wave of fascism is bespattering the Socialist movement of the working class and besmirching the democratic strivings of the best people in the civilized world, the new Constitution of the U.S.S.R. will be an indictment against fascism, declaring that Socialism and democracy are invincible. The new Constitution of the U.S.S.R. will give moral assistance and real support to all those who are today fighting fascist barbarism."*

The Socialist victories achieved by the Party served still more to infuriate the enemies of the people.

---

* J. V. Stalin, *Problems of Leninism*, Moscow 1947, p. 567.

In 1937 new facts were brought to light regarding the fiendish crimes of the Trotsky-Bukharin gang of spies, saboteurs and assassins, hirelings of the espionage services of capitalist states. The trials which followed revealed that these dregs of humanity had been conspiring against Lenin, whom they had intended to arrest, and against the Party and the Soviet State from the very first days of the October Revolution. At the bidding of their imperialist masters, they had made it their aim to destroy the Party and the Soviet State, to undermine the defence of the country, to facilitate foreign intervention, to pave the way for the defeat of the Red Army, to dismember the U.S.S.R., to convert it into a colony of imperialism and to restore capitalist slavery in the country. The Party and the Soviet Government demolished the hornets' nest of enemies of the people. In his report on "Defects in Party Work," delivered at the Plenum of the Central Committee in March 1937, Stalin outlined a clear-cut program for reinforcing the Party and Soviet bodies, and for heightening political vigilance. He advanced the slogan: "Master Bolshevism!" He armed the Party to fight the enemies of the people and taught it to tear the masks from their faces.

The Soviet courts disclosed the crimes of the Trotsky-Bukharin fiends and sentenced them to be shot. The Soviet people approved the annihilation of the Trotsky-Bukharin gang and passed on to the

J. V. Stalin in his study
Photo

next task, which was to prepare for the elections to the Supreme Soviet of the U.S.S.R.

Guided by the Central Committee and by Comrade Stalin, the Party threw all its energies into the preparations for the elections. The new Constitution signified a turn in the political life of the country, the further democratization of all its phases. The effect of the new electoral system was to enhance the political activity of the people, to strengthen the control of the masses over the organs of Soviet power, and to increase the responsibility of the latter to the people. In conformity with these new tasks, the Party, guided by the Central Committee and by Stalin, revised its methods of work, extending inner-Party democracy, strengthening the principles of democratic centralism, developing criticism and self-criticism, and increasing the responsibility of the Party bodies to the general membership. Stalin's idea of a Communist and non-Party bloc was taken by the Party as the keynote of the election campaign.

On December 11, 1937, on the eve of the elections, Stalin addressed the voters of the Stalin electoral district, Moscow. In this speech, he pointed to the fundamental difference between elections in the U.S.S.R., which are free and democratic in every sense of the word, and elections in capitalist countries, where the people are under the pressure of the exploiting classes. In the U.S.S.R. the exploiting classes had been eliminated, Socialism had become part of everyday life, and this was the basis on which the elections were taking place. Further, Stalin described the type of political figure the people should elect to the Supreme Soviet. The people must demand that they should be political figures of the Lenin type, that they should be as clear and definite, as fearless in battle, as completely immune to panic, as merciless towards the enemies of the people as Lenin was; that they should be as wise and deliberate in deciding complex political problems requiring a comprehensive orientation as Lenin was; that they should be as upright as Lenin was; that they should love their people as Lenin did.

The whole country listened to the speech of the sage and genius, their leader. His words sank deep into the minds of the working people. The speech defined the principles which should guide the activities of the deputies of the people; it fired the people with enthusiasm and still further cemented the Communist and non-Party bloc.

The elections to the Supreme Soviet of the U.S.S.R. took place on December 12. They turned into a nation-wide holiday, a celebration of the triumph of the Soviet people. Of a total of 94,000,000 voters, over 91,000,000, or 96.8 per cent, went to the polls; 90,000,000 people voted for the Communist and non-Party bloc, a fervent testimony to the victory of Socialism. This was a resounding victory for the Stalin Communist and non-Party bloc, a triumph for the Party of Lenin and Stalin, and for its Leninist-Stalinist leadership.

The moral and political unity of the Soviet people was here brilliantly confirmed. And first among the elected of the people, first among the deputies to the Supreme Soviet, was Stalin.

In view of the tremendously increased activity of the masses, and the immense problems involved in the further advancement of Socialist construction, the question of ideological and political training of our cadres acquired a new significance.

In a number of his public utterances, Comrade Stalin strongly stressed the necessity for our cadres to master Bolshevism. He pointed out that all the necessary means and opportunities were available to train our cadres ideologically and to steel them politically, and that on this depended nine-tenths of the solution of all practical problems.

In 1938, the *History of the Communist Party of the Soviet Union (Bolsheviks), Short Course,* written by Comrade Stalin, and approved by a commission of the Central Committee of the C.P.S.U.(B.), appeared.

The publication of this book was a major event in the ideological life of the Bolshevik Party. It supplied the Party with a new and powerful ideological weapon of Bolshevism, a veritable encyclopaedia of fundamental knowledge in Marxism-Leninism. Written with the lucidity and profundity characteristic of Stalin, this book provides an exposition and generalization of the vast historical experience of the Communist Party, unequalled by that of any other party in the world. The *History of the C.P.S.U.(B.)* shows the development of Marxism under the new conditions of the class struggle of the proletariat, the Marxism of the era of imperialism and proletarian revolutions, of the era of the victory of Socialism in one-sixth of the world. The book was disseminated in enormous numbers of copies in a very short period. "It may be quite definitely asserted," said Zhdanov at the Eighteenth Congress of the Party, "that this is the first Marxist book to have been disseminated so widely ever since Marxism has been in existence."

The chapter on "Dialectical and Historical Materialism" is a masterly statement of the principles of dialectical and historical materialism, expounded with the utmost conciseness and lucidity. Here Comrade Stalin summarizes all that has been contributed to the dialectical method and materialistic theory by Marx, Engels and Lenin, and further develops the teachings of dialectical and historical materialism in conformity with the latest facts of science and revolutionary practice.

He develops dialectical materialism as the theoretical foundation of Communism, as the world outlook of the Marxist-Leninist Party, the ideologi-

A meeting of the Presidium of the Supreme Soviet of the U.S.S.R.

Photo

cal weapon of the working class in its struggle to establish the dictatorship of the proletariat and to build up Communism. In this work the underlying connection between the Marxist-Leninist philosophy and the practical revolutionary activities of the Bolshevik Party is brought out very forcibly. In order to avoid mistakes in policy, Stalin teaches, we must be guided by the principles of the Marxist dialectical method and must know the laws of historical development.

J. V. Stalin's "Dialectical and Historical Materialism," written by an incomparable master of the Marxist dialectical method, and generalizing the vast practical and theoretical experience of Bolshevism, *raises dialectical materialism to a new and higher level, and is the veritable pinnacle of Marxist-Leninist philosophical thought.*

Stalin guided the labours of the Eighteenth Congress of the Party, which met in March 1939. This Congress was an imposing demonstration of the solidarity of the Party, monolithic and united as never before around the Leninist-Stalinist Central Committee.

In his report on the work of the Central Committee, Stalin gave a profound analysis of the international position of the Soviet Union and exposed the schemes of the instigators of war and intervention against the U.S.S.R. Five years had elapsed since the Seventeenth Party Congress. For the capitalist countries this had been a period of grave upheavals both in the economic and the political sphere. The economic crisis of 1929-32 and the depression of a special kind had been followed, in the latter half of 1937, by a new economic crisis, involving the U.S.A., Great Britain, France and a number of other capitalist countries. The international situation had grown acute in the extreme, the postwar system of peace treaties had suffered shipwreck, and a new, the second, world war had begun.

The new war was unleashed by the two most aggressive of the imperialist states—Germany and Japan. This war, Comrade Stalin said, had drawn over five hundred million people into its orbit and its sphere of action extended over a vast territory, stretching from Tientsin, Shanghai and Canton, through Abyssinia, to Gibraltar. The war was more and more infringing on the interests of the non-aggressive states, primarily of Great Britain, France and the U.S.A. Yet the governments of these countries were making no proper resistance to the aggressors. They had rejected a policy of collective security and assumed a position of "neutrality," of non-intervention. The policy of non-intervention was tantamount to conniving at aggression, to giving free rein to war. The sponsors of the notorious Munich agreement, the rulers of Britain and France—Chamberlain and Daladier—wanted to direct German fascist aggression eastward, against the Soviet Union.

Comrade Stalin exposed the machinations of the instigators of war against the U.S.S.R. who asserted that the Munich concessions to the aggressors and the Munich non-intervention agreement had ushered in an era of "appeasement." He warned that "the big and dangerous political game started by the supporters of the policy of non-intervention may end in a serious fiasco for them."*

In an exceptionally profound analysis, Comrade Stalin made clear to the Party and the Soviet people all the complexity and danger of the existing international situation and defined the principles of Soviet foreign policy. He said:

"The tasks of the Party in the sphere of foreign policy are:

"1. To continue the policy of peace and of strengthening business relations with all countries;

"2. To be cautious and not allow our country to be drawn into conflicts by warmongers who are accustomed to have others pull the chestnuts out of the fire for them;

"3. To strengthen the might of our Red Army and Red Navy to the utmost;

"4. To strengthen the international bonds of friendship with the working people of all countries,

---

* J. V. Stalin, *Problems of Leninism*, Moscow 1947, p. 604.

who are interested in peace and friendship among nations."*

After describing the achievements and successes of Socialism, the progress of Socialist economy, the rising material and cultural standards of the people, and the increasing consolidation of the Soviet system, Comrade Stalin put before the Party and the whole Soviet people a new and great historic task, namely, to overtake and outstrip the principal capitalist countries economically—i.e., in volume of output per head of population—in the next ten or fifteen years.

"We have outstripped the principal capitalist countries as regards technique of production and rate of industrial development," he said. "That is very good, but it is not enough. We must outstrip them economically as well. We can do it, and we must do it. Only if we outstrip the principal capitalist countries economically can we reckon upon our country being fully saturated with consumers' goods, on having an abundance of products, and on being able to make the transition from the first phase of Communism to its second phase."**

Comrade Stalin outlined, as one of the most important tasks of the Party, a complete scientifically-

___

* J. V. Stalin, *Problems of Leninism*, Moscow 1947, p. 606.

** *Ibid.*, p. 610.

grounded Bolshevik program for the training, education, selection, promotion and testing of cadres.

Reviewing the ground covered by the Party in the interval between the Seventeenth and Eighteenth Congresses, he said:

"The chief conclusion to be drawn is that the working class of our country, having abolished the exploitation of man by man and firmly established the Socialist system, has proved to the world the truth of its cause. That is the chief conclusion, for it strengthens our faith in the power of the working class and in the inevitability of its ultimate victory."*

Stalin's report to the Eighteenth Congress of the C.P.S.U.(B.) is a programmatic document of Communism, a new step in the development of Marxist-Leninist theory. Stalin carried Lenin's theory of the Socialist revolution a stage further. He gave concrete shape to the theory of the possibility of building Socialism in one country and concluded that *the building of Communism in our country was possible, even if it continued to be surrounded by a capitalist world*. This conclusion enriches Leninism, arms the working class with a new ideological weapon, opens up to the Party the majestic prospect of a struggle for the victory of Communism, and advances the theory of Marxism-Leninism.

---

* *Ibid.*, p. 641.

145

Lenin wrote his famous work *The State and Revolution* in August 1917, a few months prior to the October Revolution and the establishment of the Soviet State. In this book, Lenin defended Marx's and Engels' teaching regarding the state against the distortions and vulgarizations of the opportunists. It was Lenin's intention to write a second volume of *The State and Revolution*, in which he meant to sum up the principal lessons of the Russian revolutions of 1905 and 1917. Death, however, prevented Lenin from accomplishing his design. That which Lenin had not lived to do in development of the theory of the state, was done by Stalin.

Drawing on the vast experience accumulated during the more than twenty years the Soviet Socialist State had existed in the midst of a capitalist world, Comrade Stalin developed an *integral and complete theory of the Socialist State*. He made a detailed analysis of the stages of development of the Socialist State and of the way its functions changed with changes in conditions; he summarized the experience accumulated in the building of the Soviet State, and arrived at the conclusion that the state would have to be preserved under Communism if the capitalist encirclement persisted.

Stalin stressed the momentous importance of Party propaganda and the Marxist-Leninist education of the functionaries of the Party and the Young Communist League, of the trade unions and trade, cooperative, and economic organizations, and of government, educational, military and other bodies.

"If," he said, "the Marxist-Leninist training of our cadres begins to languish, if our work of raising the political and theoretical level of these cadres flags, and the cadres themselves cease on account of this to show interest in the prospect of our further progress, cease to understand the truth of our cause and are transformed into narrow plodders with no outlook, blindly and mechanically carrying out instructions from above—then our entire state and Party work must inevitably languish. It must be accepted as an axiom that the higher the political level and the Marxist-Leninist knowledge of the workers in any branch of state or Party work, the better and more fruitful will be the work itself, and the more effective the results of the work; and, vice versa, the lower the political level of the workers, and the less they are imbued with knowledge of Marxism-Leninism, the greater will be the likelihood of disruption and failure in the work, of the workers themselves becoming shallow and deteriorating into paltry plodders, of their degenerating altogether. It may be confidently stated that if we succeeded in training the cadres in all branches of our work ideologically, and in schooling them politically, to such an extent as to enable them easily to orientate themselves in the internal and international situation; if we succeeded in making them quite mature Marxist-Leninists capable of solving the problems involved in the guidance of the country without serious error, we would have every reason to consider nine-tenths of our problems already settled. And we certainly can accomplish this, for we have all the means and opportunities for doing so."*

Stalin further said: "There is one branch of science which Bolsheviks in all branches of science are in duty bound to know, and that is the Marxist-Leninist science of society, of the laws of social development, of the laws of development of the proletarian revolution, of the laws of development of Socialist construction, and of the victory of Communism. For a man who calls himself a Leninist cannot be considered a real Leninist if he shuts himself up in his speciality, in mathematics, botany or chemistry, let us say, and sees nothing beyond that speciality. A Leninist cannot be just a specialist in his favourite science; he must also be a political and social worker, keenly interested in the destinies of his country, acquainted with the laws of social development, capable of applying these laws, and striving to be an active participant in the political guidance of the country. This, of course, will be an additional burden on specialists who are Bolsheviks. But it will a burden more than compensated for by its results.

* J. V. Stalin, *Problems of Leninism*, Moscow 1947, pp. 629-30.

"The task of Party propaganda, the task of the Marxist-Leninist training of cadres, is to help our cadres in all branches of work to become versed in the Marxist-Leninist science of the laws of social development."*

Comrade Stalin's report to the Eighteenth Congress of the C.P.S.U.(B.) was a program for the completion of the building of a classless Socialist society and for the gradual transition from Socialism to Communism. The Congress unanimously endorsed the report of the Party leader as a directive and a law to the Party in all its activities.

The report was a brilliant example of scientific, Marxist-Leninist foresight in the sphere of international relations. Stalin's wise instructions on the aims of Soviet foreign policy, and his skill in leadership, resulted in major victories for Soviet foreign policy and enhanced the prestige of the Soviet Union as a serious international force, able to influence the international situation and to change it in the interests of the working people. Guided by Comrade Stalin's recommendations, the Soviet Government thwarted the perfidious schemes of the instigators of war who were keen on having other people pull the chestnuts out of the fire for them, and safeguarded the peaceful labour of the peoples of the U.S.S.R. The mutual assistance pacts concluded by the Soviet

* *Ibid.*, p. 630.

Union with the Baltic States immeasurably strengthened the defences of the Socialist country and its
international position.

The Soviet Government strove to prevent the
further spread of war and to promote a policy of
collective security. But this policy found no support
among the ruling circles of Great Britain and France.
The Munich policy of non-intervention turned out
to be a costly thing for the peoples of the non-aggressive countries. In March 1939, with the connivance
of British and French diplomacy, Hitler Germany
seized Czechoslovakia. This was soon followed by
an offensive of the German aggressors against the
countries of Eastern Europe. Imperialist Japan—
Germany's ally in the Far East—also became active.
In May 1939, she launched a series of provocative
sorties on the frontier of the Mongolian People's
Republic, but at Khalkhin-gol the Japanese Manchu-
rian army suffered signal defeat at the hands of
the Red Army.

British and French diplomacy, meanwhile, was
playing dishonestly towards the U.S.S.R., deliberately
protracting negotiations with it for the organization
of collective resistance to a possible aggressor, and
proposing conditions for the conclusion of an agreement which were clearly unacceptable to the Soviet
Union.

Seeing that Britain and France were not disposed
to cooperate with the U.S.S.R. for the maintenance

of peace, the Soviet Government had to give thought to safeguarding the security of our country.

In August 1939, the Government of the U.S.S.R. concluded a treaty of non-aggression with Germany. This treaty, as Comrade Stalin subsequently stated, did not jeopardize, either directly or indirectly, the territorial integrity, independence and honour of the Soviet Union. But it did ensure it peace for some time and the opportunity to prepare its forces for resistance in the event of attack.

Bearing in mind Comrade Stalin's insistence on the necessity of maintaining the country in a state of mobilized readiness against the contingency of armed foreign attack, the Bolshevik Party had for a long time been working consistently and undeviatingly to put the Soviet Union in a state of all-round readiness for active defence. The Soviet policy of industrialization and of collectivization of agriculture carried out during the period of the Stalin five-year plans had created a powerful economic base capable of being utilized for the active defence of the country.

This policy of the Party had made it possible to produce domestically sufficient metal for the manufacture of weapons, equipment and ammunition, machinery and fuel for the factories and the railways, cotton for making army clothing, and food for the supply of the armed forces.

Thanks to the policy of industrializing the country and collectivizing agriculture, the Soviet Union

In 1940 produced: 15,000,000 tons of pig iron, or nearly four times as much as tsarist Russia produced in 1913; 18,300,000 tons of steel, or four and a half times as much as in 1913; 166,000,000 tons of coal, or five and a half times as much as in 1913; 31,000,000 tons of oil, or three and a half times as much as in 1913; 38,300,000 tons of marketable grain, or 17,000,000 tons more than in 1913; 2,700,000 tons of raw cotton, or three and a half times as much as in 1913.

"This unprecedented growth of production," Comrade Stalin said, "cannot be regarded as the simple and ordinary development of a country from backwardness to progress. It was a leap by which our Motherland became transformed from a backward into an advanced country, from an agrarian into an industrial country."*

In the autumn of 1939, on Comrade Stalin's initiative, our brothers by blood, the peoples of the Western Ukraine and Western Byelorussia, were delivered from the yoke of the Polish landlords. These peoples merged with the united family of free nations of the U.S.S.R. In August 1940 the Soviet Baltic Republics—Lithuania, Latvia and Estonia—were restored to the U.S.S.R.

---

* J. V. Stalin, *Speech Delivered at an Election Meeting in the Stalin Electoral District, Moscow, February 9, 1946,* Russ. ed., p. 15.

J. V. STALIN

Photo

On December 20, 1939, on the occasion of his sixtieth birthday, J. V. Stalin, by decision of the Presidium of the Supreme Soviet of the U.S.S.R., was granted the title of Hero of Socialist Labour in recognition of his outstanding services in the organization of the Bolshevik Party, the creation of the Soviet state, the building of Socialist society in the U.S.S.R., and in strengthening the ties of mutual friendship of the Soviet peoples.

On December 22, 1939, Comrade Stalin was elected an honorary member of the Academy of Sciences of the U.S.S.R.

The Eighteenth All-Union Conference of the C.P.S.U.(B.) was held on February 15-20, 1941. It discussed the tasks of the Party organizations in industry and transport, the economic results of the year 1910, the plan for the economic development of the U.S.S.R. in 1941, and organizational questions.

The keynote of the Conference, set by Comrade Stalin, was the further strengthening of the defensive power of the Soviet Union.

On Comrade Stalin's initiative, the Central Committee of the C.P.S.U.(B.) and the Soviet Government instructed the State Planning Commission of the U.S.S.R. to proceed to draw up a general economic plan for the country covering a period of fifteen years, based on the decisions of the Eighteenth Party Congress. The objective of the plan was to overtake the principal capitalist countries economically, that is, in output per head of the population of iron, steel, fuel, electric power, machines and other means of production and articles of consumption.

On May 6, 1941, J. V. Stalin, by decision of the Presidium of the Supreme Soviet of the U.S.S.R., was appointed Chairman of the Council of People's Commissars of the U.S.S.R.

Led by the great Stalin, the Soviet people were marching toward new victories, toward Communism. But in June 1941, Germany attacked the U.S.S.R., and war interrupted the peaceful constructive labours of the Soviet people.

★

XI

ON JUNE 22, 1941, imperialist Hitler Germany, in gross violation of the pact of non-aggression, treacherously and without warning attacked the Soviet Union. This turned the whole course of development of the Soviet country. The period of peaceful construction had come to an end, and a period of war began—a Patriotic War of liberation waged by the Soviet people against the German invaders.

To ensure the rapid mobilization of all the forces of the peoples of the U.S.S.R. for the repulsion of the enemy, the Presidium of the Supreme Soviet of the U.S.S.R., the Central Committee of the C.P.S.U. (B.) and the Council of People's Commissars of the U.S.S.R. decided on June 30, 1941, to set up a State Committee of Defence, in whose hands all power in the state was concentrated. Joseph Vissarionovich Stalin was appointed Chairman of the Committee.

The leader and teacher of the working people, Comrade Stalin, took command of the armed forces of the U.S.S.R. and led the struggle of the Soviet people against a malignant and treacherous enemy, German fascism.

Hitler Germany had many advantages when she launched her war of plunder and aggrandizement against the U.S.S.R. Her army was fully mobilized and had already had experience in warfare in Western Europe. One hundred and seventy German divisions, supported by thousands of tanks and aircraft, had been moved up to the frontiers of the U.S.S.R. and were suddenly hurled against the Land of Soviets. In the early stages of the war the armed forces of the peace-loving Soviet Union were therefore at a disadvantage. Under the pressure of the numerically superior forces and armament of the enemy, who made full use of the advantage of a surprise attack, the Soviet Army was forced to beat a fighting retreat deeper and deeper into the country.

In the first ten days of the war, Hitler's troops succeeded in capturing Lithuania, a considerable part of Latvia, the Western part of Byelorussia and part of the Western Ukraine. Grave danger overhung the Soviet Union.

On July 3, 1941, Comrade Stalin addressed the Soviet people and the men of the Red Army and Navy over the radio. It was a historic speech. He gave a profound analysis of the events, and defined the tasks of the armed forces and the people in defending the Socialist Motherland.

Comrade Stalin told the stern truth about the military situation; he called upon the Soviet people to appreciate the full immensity of the danger menacing the Motherland, and to cast off the mentality of the period of peaceful constructive work. He warned that complacency and heedlessness must be put aside, there must be no fear in the fight, and no room for whimperers, panicmongers or deserters.

He disclosed Hitler Germany's aims in her war against the Soviet Union: "The enemy is cruel and implacable. He is out to seize our lands which have been watered by the sweat of our brow, to seize our grain and oil which have been obtained by the labour of our hands. He is out to restore the rule of the landlords, to restore tsarism, to destroy the national culture and the national existence as states of the Russians, Ukrainians, Byelorussians, Lithuanians, Latvians, Estonians, Uzbeks, Tatars, Moldavians, Georgians, Armenians, Azerbaijanians and the other free peoples of the Soviet Union, to Germanize them, to convert them into the slaves of German princes and barons. Thus, the issue is one of life and death for the Soviet State, of life and death for the peoples of the U.S.S.R., of whether the peoples of the Soviet Union shall be free or fall into slavery."*

Comrade Stalin also defined the aims of the Soviet Union in the war against fascist Germany. He said that it was a great war of the entire Soviet people

---

* J. V. Stalin, *On the Great Patriotic War of the Soviet Union*, Moscow 1946, p. 13.

against the German fascist army. The aim of this people's Patriotic War was not only to remove the danger hanging over the country, but also to aid all the European peoples who were groaning under the yoke of German fascism.

He prophesied that in this war of liberation the Soviet people would not be alone. "Our war for the freedom of our Motherland will merge with the struggle of the peoples of Europe and America for their independence, for the democratic liberties. It will be a united front of the peoples who stand for freedom and against enslavement and threats of enslavement by Hitler's fascist armies."*

Events confirmed the truth of Comrade Stalin's prophecy. On July 12, 1941, Great Britain concluded with the U.S.S.R. an Agreement for Joint Action in the War Against Germany. Later (June 1942), the U.S.A. signed with the U.S.S.R. an Agreement on the Principles Applicable to Mutual Aid in the Prosecution of the War Against Aggression. An Anglo-Soviet-American coalition was formed for the purpose of destroying the Italo-German coalition.

Comrade Stalin called upon the Soviet people to reorganize all their work on a war footing and to subordinate everything to the needs of the front and the task of organizing the defeat of the enemy. The

---

* J. V. Stalin, *On the Great Patriotic War of the Soviet Union*, Moscow 1946. p. 16.

Red Army and Navy and all citizens of the Soviet Union, he said, must defend every inch of Soviet soil, must fight to the last drop of blood for every town and village. He spoke of the necessity of organizing all-round assistance to the Red Army, of strengthening its rear and supplying it with weapons, ammunition and food.

He gave orders that in case of Red Army units having to make a forced retreat, not a single locomotive or railway car, nor a single pound of grain or gallon of fuel should be left for the enemy. He called for the formation of guerilla units and the combination of a guerilla war in the enemy's rear with the operations of the Red Army.

And Comrade Stalin ended his address with the call:

"All forces of the people for routing the enemy!

"Forward to victory!"

All the nations of the Soviet Union rose up in response to the Party's call to defend the Motherland.

The entire national economy and the work of all Party, government and public organizations were rapidly and resolutely put on a war footing to meet the needs of the armed forces. Front and rear became a single and indivisible armed camp. The entire Soviet people united and rallied around the Bolshevik Party and the Government as never before.

Very soon, the entire industry of the country was converted for the production of defence material. Thousands of plants were evacuated from the areas threatened by the enemy into the heart of the country and continued to operate there. The building of new war plants was effectively developed in the Eastern regions of the country. Replenishments poured into the Red Army. A volunteer home guard was formed in the cities and rural districts of the war areas. In the Soviet territories seized by the enemy gallant guerillas—the people's avengers—began to operate from the first days of the war.

On July 19, 1941, the Presidium of the Supreme Soviet of the U.S.S.R. appointed J. V. Stalin People's Commissar of Defence. He worked might and main to strengthen the armed forces of the Soviet Union. Under his direction the Soviet Army adopted the tactics of active defence, with the object of wearing down the enemy's strength and destroying as much as possible of his man power and materiel, and thus paving the way for an assumption of the offensive.

The Hitler command counted on a lightning victory over the U.S.S.R. and the swift seizure of Moscow and Leningrad, and hurled their reserves into the Soviet-German front, heedless of the huge losses in men and armament which the German army was sustaining. In October, at the cost of immense casualties, the Germans managed to break through to the Moscow Region.

This was the most dangerous moment in the
campaign of 1941. Mortal danger threatened Moscow.
On October 19, 1941, an order was published by
Comrade Stalin, as Chairman of the State Committee
of Defence, proclaiming a state of siege in Moscow.
Stalin worked out and brilliantly carried into effect
a plan for the defence of the capital and for the
ultimate defeat of the German armies at Moscow.

The enemy was already at the approaches to the
city. Notwithstanding this, on November 6, 1941, the
traditional meeting of the Moscow Soviet of Working
People's Deputies and representatives of the Moscow
Party and public organizations was held in the city
to celebrate the anniversary, the 24th, of the Great
October Socialist Revolution. The meeting was addressed by Comrade Stalin.

He reviewed the four months of the war. The
leader of the army and the people was austere and
forthright. He warned that the grave danger over-
hanging the country had by no means abated, and
in fact was greater than ever. Yet, with his supreme
insight, he foresaw that the defeat of the German
imperialists and their armies was inevitable.

The plan of the German fascist invaders to
"finish off" the Soviet Union by a blitzkrieg in the
course of one and a half or two months had definitely failed. The hopes of the German fascist strate-
gists to create a universal coalition against the
U.S.S.R. and to isolate it, their belief that the Soviet

system was unstable, that the Soviet rear was unsound, and that the Red Army and Navy were weak, had proved unfounded.

Comrade Stalin disclosed the reasons for the temporary reverses of the Red Army. One of them was the absence of a second front in Europe. Another was that the Red Army was inadequately supplied with tanks, and to some extent with aircraft, although its tanks and aircraft were superior in quality to those of the Germans.

The task, Comrade Stalin said, was to nullify the Germans' numerical superiority in tanks and aircraft and thus radically improve the position of our army.

This directive of the leader had an immense influence in determining the ultimate issue of the war. Following this directive, Soviet industry each month produced more aircraft and tanks and anti-aircraft and anti-tank weapons, and in due course the enemy's superiority in armament was nullified.

Comrade Stalin tore away the mask of "National-Socialism" and exposed the Hitlerites as a party of the most rapacious imperialists in the world, as enemies of the democratic liberties, as a party of medieval reactionaries and Black Hundred pogrom-mongers, of assassins who had lost all human semblance and sunk to the level of wild beasts.

"And these men," Stalin said, "destitute of conscience and honour, these men with the morals of beasts, have the insolence to call for the extermina-

162

tion of the great Russian nation, the nation of Plekhanov and Lenin, Belinsky and Chernyshevsky, Pushkin and Tolstoy, Glinka and Chaikovsky, Gorky and Chekhov, Secherov and Pavlov, Repin and Surikov, Suvorov and Kutuzov!..."[*]

Comrade Stalin called upon the Soviet people to intensify their efforts in support of the army and navy, to work selflessly in support of the front. The German fascist invaders must be exterminated, he said. "The German invaders want a war of extermination against the peoples of the U.S.S.R. Well, if the Germans want a war of extermination, they will get it. "[**]

"Ours is a just cause—victory will be ours!"[***] These words of Stalin expressed the thoughts and aspirations of all Soviet people and their deep confidence that the enemy would be vanquished.

The following day, November 7, a Red Army Parade was held on the Red Square in Moscow. Stalin spoke from Lenin's Mausoleum. He told of the Red Army's great liberating mission, and urged on the armed forces and the men and women of the guerilla detachments with the words: "Let the heroic images of our great forebears—Alexander Nevsky,

---

[*] J. V. Stalin, *On the Great Patriotic War of the Soviet Union*, Moscow 1946, pp. 30-31.

[**] *Ibid.*, p. 31.

[***] *Ibid.*, p. 37.

Dimitry Donskoy, Kuzma Minin, Dimitry Pozharsky, Alexander Suvorov and Mikhail Kutuzov—inspire you in this war! May you be inspired by the victorious banner of the Great Lenin!"*

The Red Army responded to the words of its leader with an access of staunchness and determination, and by redoubling the force of its blows at the enemy.

Comrade Stalin personally directed the defence of Moscow and the operations of the Red Army; he inspired men and commanders, and supervised the building of the defence works at the approaches to the Soviet capital.

On December 6, 1941, on Comrade Stalin's orders, several Soviet armies which had been concentrated around Moscow suddenly struck at the enemy. After stern and heavy fighting, the Germans crumbled under the assault and began to retire in disorder. The Soviet troops drove the routed Germans before them and that winter advanced westward, in places over 400 kilometres. Hitler's plan for the encirclement and capture of Moscow ended in a fiasco.

The rout of the German fascist armies at Moscow was the decisive military event in the first year of the war and the first big defeat the Germans had sustained in World War II. It dispelled once and for

* J. V. Stalin, *On the Great Patriotic War of the Soviet Union*, Moscow 1946, p. 41.

all the Hitlerite legend that the German army was invincible.

The German rout at Moscow demonstrated the superiority of the strategical plan of offence worked out by Stalin over the German strategy.

In his Order of the Day No. 55, of February 23, 1942, J. V. Stalin stressed, as the major result of the first eight months of the war, the fact that the Germans had lost the military advantage they had possessed in consequence of their treacherous surprise attack on the U.S.S.R.

"The element of surprise and suddenness, as a reserve of the German fascist troops, is completely spent. This removes the inequality in fighting conditions created by the suddenness of the German fascist attack. Now the outcome of the war will be decided not by such a fortuitous element as surprise, but by permanently operating factors: stability of the rear, morale of the army, quantity and quality of divisions, equipment of the army and organizing ability of the commanding personnel of the army."*

Stalin's thesis regarding the significance of the permanently operating factors of war, as the decisive factors, was a constructive development of the Marxist-Leninist science of warfare, which stresses the direct and organic connection between the course and outcome of war and the degree and character

_____

* *Ibid.*, p. 45.

of the economic and political development of the states concerned, their ideologies, and the training and maturity of their human forces.

Stalin's thesis regarding the role of the permanently operating factors is of paramount theoretical and practical importance. Proper consideration for and utilization of the permanently operating factors make it possible in military operations and matters of organization to focus chief attention on the basic problems on which the issue of war depends.

Comrade Stalin attaches great importance to the proper mastery of the art of war by commanders and men. In his Order of the Day of May 1, 1942, he pointed out that the Red Army now possessed all that was needed to defeat the enemy and drive him out of the Soviet Union. But "it lacks only one thing —the ability to utilize to the full against the enemy the first-class materiel with which our country supplies it. Hence, it is the task of the Red Army, of its men, of its machine-gunners, its artillerymen, its mortarmen, its tankmen, its airmen and its cavalrymen to study the art of war, to study assiduously, to study the mechanism of their weapons to perfection, to become expert at their jobs and thus learn to strike the enemy with unerring aim. Only thus can the art of defeating the enemy be learnt."*

_____

* J. V. Stalin, *On the Great Patriotic War of the Soviet Union*, Moscow 1946, p. 59.

And all through the subsequent course of the war Comrade Stalin constantly insisted on the necessity of perfecting military training, of increasing knowledge and the ability to utilize the mechanisms of war, and of mastering the art of command, of beating the enemy in accordance with all the rules of the modern science of warfare. The Red Army took these instructions to heart and stubbornly and persistently studied the job of war, and learned to beat the enemy unerringly.

In the summer of 1942, taking advantage of the absence of a second front in Europe, the Germans transferred all their reserves, including the armies of their allies, to the Soviet front and massed huge forces in the southwestern sector.

Comrade Stalin promptly divined the plan of the German command. He saw that the idea was to create the impression that the seizure of the oil regions of Grozny and Baku was the major and not a subsidiary objective of the German summer offensive. He pointed out that in reality the main objective was to envelop Moscow from the East, to cut it off from its rear, the areas of the Volga and Urals, then to strike at Moscow, and in this way end the war in 1942.

The Soviet troops were ordered by Supreme Commander-in-Chief Stalin to bar the enemy's march northward, into Moscow's rear. In the middle of July 1942 the Germans launched an offensive against

Stalingrad, calculating to take the city on the run, to tear open the Soviet front, and then to continue their advance northward along the Volga, outflanking Moscow. Comrade Stalin gave instructions that Stalingrad should be held at all costs. On October 5, 1942, he sent an order to the commander of the Stalingrad Front saying: "I demand that you take all measures for the defence of Stalingrad. Stalingrad must not be surrendered to the enemy."*

The Battle of Stalingrad, the biggest engagement in history, began. The Red Army heroically defended the famous city on the Volga that bears Stalin's name. The fighting traditions of the Tsaritsyn epic of 1918 were revived. At the height of the battle, the men, commanders and political officers of the Stalingrad Front sent a letter to Stalin, every word of which sounded like a solemn vow. "Before our battle standards and the whole Soviet country, we swear that we will not besmirch the glory of Russian arms and will fight to the last. Under your leadership, our fathers won the Battle of Tsaritsyn, and under your leadership we will now win the great Battle of Stalingrad."**

It was at a time when the enemy had broken through to Stalingrad and the foothills of the Caucasus that the Soviet Union celebrated the 25th an-

---

* *Pravda*, No. 28, February 2, 1944.
** *Pravda*, No. 310, November 6, 1942.

niversary of the Great October Socialist Revolution. On November 6, 1942, at the celebration meeting of the Moscow Soviet, Stalin again addressed the people.

He reviewed in detail what had been done by the government and Party bodies in the past year both in the sphere of peaceful construction and the organization of a strong rear for the armed forces, and in the sphere of conducting the defensive and offensive operations of the Red Army.

Comrade Stalin spoke of the supremely difficult and complicated organizational work that had been accomplished during the war in transplanting defence and civilian industries to the Eastern regions of the country and reconstructing and radically improving the work of the industries supplying the armed forces. "It must be admitted," Comrade Stalin said, "that never before has our ountry had such a strong and well-organized rear."*

Comrade Stalin explained why the Germans had been able to score substantial tactical successes in the summer of 1942. It was because the absence of a second front in Europe had enabled them to create a big superiority of forces in the southwestern sector.

Examining the question of a second front in Europe from the historical angle, Comrade Stalin

---

* J. V. Stalin, *On the Great Patriotic War of the Soviet Union*, Moscow 1946, p. 64.

cited the following significant figures: in World War I, Germany, which was then fighting on two fronts, brought against the Russian front 127 divisions, including the divisions of her allies. In this war, Germany, which was fighting only on one front, had hurled against the Soviet front 240 divisions, or nearly twice as many as in World War I.

It was only the heroism of the Soviet Army and the guerillas, only the devoted labour of the Soviet patriots in the rear and the proper direction of Comrade Stalin as Supreme Commander-in-Chief of the Armed Forces and leader of the Party and of the Soviet State, that had made it possible to cope with the gigantic difficulties involved in resisting the onslaught of Hitler's hordes. With a feeling of supreme pride in the Soviet country, the Soviet people and its army, Comrade Stalin said:

"I think that no other country and no other army could have withstood this onslaught of the savage gangs of German fascist brigands and their allies. Only our Soviet country and only our Red Army are capable of withstanding such an onslaught. And not only withstanding it, but also overpowering it."*

The task Comrade Stalin set before the Red Army was to prevent the enemy from advancing

---

* J. V. Stalin, *On the Great Patriotic War of the Soviet Union*, Moscow 1946, p. 72.

further, and meanwhile stubbornly and persistently to prepare to strike back at him.

This speech of their leader and military commander was hailed with intense enthusiasm by the Red Army and the entire Soviet people. The millions of workers and collective farmers still further increased the output of munitions and food for the armed forces. A country-wide movement began for the collection of funds for the Red Army, initiated by men and women collective farmers of the Tambov Region.

Unwavering confidence in victory was infused into the hearts of the Soviet people by the words of People's Commissar of Defence Stalin in his Order of the Day of November 7, 1942: "The enemy has already felt the weight of the Red Army's blows at Rostov, Moscow and Tikhvin. The day is not far distant when the enemy will again feel the weight of the Red Army's blows. Our turn will come!"*

These words were soon to be brilliantly confirmed by the rout of the Germans at Stalingrad.

The wise leader of armies, with whose name on their lips the Soviet soldiers went into battle, foresaw the development of events and bent the course of the gigantic battle to his iron will.

* *Ibid.*, p. 83.

171

On November 19, 1942, acting on Stalin's orders, the Soviet troops at the approaches to Stalingrad passed to the offensive. They struck at the German's flanks, and then in their rear. This strategical plan of flank attacks, worked out by Comrade Stalin and carried out under his direction, ensured another resounding victory for the Red Army. Very soon, a German army 300,000 strong was surrounded in the Stalingrad area and partly annihilated and partly taken prisoner.

This was the most outstanding victory in all the great wars of history. The Battle of Stalingrad was a crowning achievement of the military art and a new demonstration of the perfection attained by the advanced Soviet science of war. This historic victory was a striking triumph for Stalin's strategy and tactics, a triumph for the wisdom and perspicacity of the plan of the great military genius, who had seen through the enemy's designs and turned the weaknesses of his reckless strategy to good account.

The significance of Stalingrad was later summed up by Stalin in the words: "Stalingrad marked the beginning of the decline of the German fascist army. It is common knowledge that the Germans never recovered from the Stalingrad slaughter."*

---

* J. V. Stalin, *On the Great Patriotic War of the Soviet Union*, Moscow 1946, p. 116.

Having seized the initiative in the Stalingrad battle, the Soviet Army continued to press its offensive. The wholesale expulsion of the enemy from the Land of the Soviets began.

In his Order of the Day of February 23, 1943, speaking of the successes of the Soviet troops and the heroism of the Soviet people, Comrade Stalin said: "Our people will forever remember the heroic defence of Sevastopol and Odessa, the stubborn battles near Moscow and in the foothills of the Caucasus, in the region of Rzhev and near Leningrad, and the greatest battle ever fought in history at the walls of Stalingrad. In these great battles our gallant men, commanders and political instructors covered the banners of the Red Army with unfading glory and laid a firm foundation for victory over the German fascist armies."*

At the same time, the Supreme Commander-in-Chief warned the men and commanders of the Soviet Army against the danger of the self-pride that comes from success. He bade them firmly to bear in mind the behest of the great Lenin: "The primary thing is not to become intoxicated by victory and not to boast; the second is to consolidate the victory; the third is to give the enemy the finishing stroke."**

---

* *Ibid.*, p. 93.
** *Ibid.*, p. 98.

The outcome of the offensive campaign of the winter of 1942-43 was that the Soviet troops not only nullified the tactical successes gained by the enemy in the summer of 1942, but also began to liberate the regions seized by the Germans at the beginning of the war.

The Soviet State marked its high appreciation of the outstanding services of the Supreme Commander-in-Chief of the Armed Forces of the U.S.S.R. when, on March 6, 1943, the Presidium of the Supreme Soviet of the U.S.S.R. conferred on Comrade Stalin the rank of Marshal of the Soviet Union.

Notwithstanding their defeats and immense losses, the Germans undertook a new offensive in the summer of 1943. Comrade Stalin saw through the enemy's plan in good time: it was to strike a blow from two directions, from the Orel and Belgorod areas, to surround and annihilate the Soviet forces in the Kursk salient, and then to launch an offensive on Moscow.

On July 2, Comrade Stalin warned the command in the Orel-Kursk sector that the Germans would probably attack some time between July 3 and 6. And when, on July 5, large forces of Nazi troops started an offensive in the Orel-Kursk and Belgorod sectors, they met with fierce resistance from the Soviet troops. The Germans' offensive proved too weak to overcome the Soviet defence, and their plan collapsed.

The sequel to this celebrated Battle of Kursk was that the Soviet troops, having worn down and decimated the crack fascist divisions, broke through the enemy's front and themselves passed to the offensive.

On July 24, Supreme Commander-in-Chief Marshal of the Soviet Union J. V. Stalin issued an order of the day announcing the definite liquidation of the Germans' July offensive. It declared that the German summer offensive plan had completely collapsed, "thereby exploding the legend that the Germans in summer are always successful in offensive operations and the Soviet troops are compelled to retreat."*

The Soviet Army successfully continued its advance. On August 5, 1943, Orel and Belgorod were retaken. Marshal Stalin paid tribute to this new outstanding victory in a special order of the day. A salute of guns in Moscow, the capital of our country, honoured the gallant troops who had liberated Orel and Belgorod. Since then salutes of guns in Moscow became a wartime tradition.

The defeat of the Germans at Kursk had a decisive influence on the whole subsequent course of the war. "If the Battle of Stalingrad presaged

---

* *Pravda*, No. 185, July 25, 1943.

the decline of the German fascist army," Stalin said, "the Battle of Kursk brought it to the brink of disaster."*

The Battle of Kursk and the liquidation of the Germans' Orel salient heralded a new powerful advance of the Soviet Army. By November 1943, two-thirds of the Soviet territories which had been seized by the enemy were liberated.

On November 6, 1943, the Presidium of the Supreme Soviet of the U.S.S.R. conferred on Comrade Stalin the Order of Suvorov, 1st Class, for the successes achieved by his masterly direction of the operations of the Red Army in the Patriotic War against the German invaders.

Valuable assistance was rendered to the Soviet armies in the 1943 offensive by the guerillas. Comrade Stalin's appeal "to fan the flames of popular guerilla warfare in the enemy's rear, destroy the enemy's bases and exterminate the German fascist scoundrels,** had given the fillip to a powerful guerilla movement. Guerillas were very active in the Germans' rear, destroying their communications and annihilating fascist officers and men. Stalin directed the movement and summoned conferences of guerilla commanders in Moscow.

---

* J. V. Stalin, *On the Great Patriotic War of the Soviet Union*, Moscow 1946, p. 117.

** *Ibid.*, p. 83.

J. V. STALIN

Drawing by B. Karpov

Comrade Stalin painted a majestic picture of the victories scored by the Soviet people and its army in the speech he delivered on November 6, 1943, at the meeting of the Moscow Soviet in celebration of the 26th anniversary of the Great Socialist Revolution.

The year 1943, he said, "marked the decisive turn in the course of the Patriotic War."*

"The results and consequences of the Red Army's victories are felt far beyond the Soviet-German front; they have changed the whole course of the World War and have acquired great international importance."**

The victories of the Soviet troops still further strengthened the international position of the U.S.S.R. The year 1943 marked a turning point not only in the Patriotic War of the Soviet Union, but in the World War generally. The Red Army's 1943 offensive was supported by the operations of the Allied forces in North Africa and in Italy and by the bombing of Germany's war industrial centres by Allied air forces. Germany's principal ally, fascist Italy, soon collapsed militarily and politically, and in September 1943 unconditionally surrendered. This was a serious blow to the Hitler coalition.

---

* *Ibid.*, p. 113.
** *Ibid.*, p. 125.

The enemy's efforts to sow dissension among the Great Powers that had united to smash Hitler Germany were foiled by the wisdom of Stalin's foreign policy. At the conference of the heads of the three Allied Powers in November 1943 in Teheran, where Comrade Stalin met the President of the United States and the Prime Minister of Great Britain, a declaration was adopted on joint action in the war against Germany and on postwar cooperation of the three Powers.

The year 1943 also marked a turning point in the work of the Soviet rear. The smoothly functioning and rapidly expanding war industry created by the efforts of the people ensured the Soviet Army a quantitative and qualitative superiority in armament over the Germans. Guided by Comrade Stalin's direct instructions, Soviet designers worked fruitfully perfecting weapons and creating new types of armament.

The Soviet Union was not only fighting; in the midst of war it was also building. The construction of new mills and factories, mines, blast furnaces and power stations continued uninterruptedly. New iron and steel mills were started in Chelyabinsk and in Uzbekistan, blast furnaces were erected at Tagil, Magnitogorsk and other places. A new aluminium plant began operation in Stalinsk, and power stations in Chelyabinsk, Stalinsk and many other parts.

Comrade Stalin encouraged the personnel in industry to greater efforts in speeding the construction and operation of new mills and factories. In December 1943 he congratulated the builders and workers of the Magnitogorsk Iron and Steel Works on the record speed with which they erected a large blast furnace amid the difficult conditions of wartime. He also paid tribute to the personnel of the Yenakievo Iron and Steel Works. Congratulating them on their achievements, he said that they were a proof that "the difficult task of rehabilitating industry and eliminating the consequences of the barbaric depredations of the Germans could be accomplished in a very short space of time."*

Comrade Stalin gave exceptionally great attention to economic rehabilitation in the areas liberated by the Soviet Army. On his initiative, the Council of People's Commissars of the U.S.S.R. and the Central Committee of the Communist Party, in August 1943, adopted a decision on "Urgent Measures for the Economic Rehabilitation of the Areas Liberated From German Occupation."

The Soviet people heroically supported the operations of their armed forces. Comrade Stalin described the devoted efforts of the Soviet people in the rear, the yeoman service rendered by the working class, the collective farmers and the intelli-

---

* *Pravda*, No. 321, December 31, 1943.

gentsia in the war, as an unparalleled feat of valour in defence of the Motherland.

In the course of the Patriotic War the mutual friendship of the nations of the Soviet Union was still further cemented. They all rose solidly in defence of their country.

In March 1944, the Supreme Soviet of the U.S.S.R., on Comrade Stalin's recommendation, adopted a decision to convert the People's Commissariat of Defence and the People's Commissariat of Foreign Affairs from Union to Union-Republican Commissariats and to form People's Commissariats of Defence and of Foreign Affairs of the Union Republics.

This was another step in the solution of the national problem in the U.S.S.R., a further development of Lenin's and Stalin's policy, which ensures the successful development of the statehood of all the nations of the Soviet Union.

The year 1944 was a year of decisive victories for the Soviet Army. Acting on a plan conceived by Stalin's strategical genius, it struck a series of ten powerful blows at the German armies. Comrade Stalin described these blows in detail in his speech on the occasion of the 27th anniversary of the Great October Socialist Revolution. As a result of these blows, all the regions of the Soviet Union which had been occupied by the German fascist invaders had now been fully liberated and the enemy driven out of the borders of the Soviet country. The Soviet Army had carried the war into the territories of Germany and her associates.

On June 20, 1944, the Chairman of the Executive Committee of the Moscow City Soviet, on behalf of the Presidium of the Supreme Soviet of the U.S.S.R., tendered the first Moscow Defence Medal to Marshal of the Soviet Union J. V. Stalin, Chairman of the State Committee of Defence and Supreme Commander-in-Chief, conferred on him in recognition of his services in directing the heroic defence of Moscow and organizing the rout of the German forces outside the Soviet capital. The ceremony took place in the Kremlin.

On July 29, 1944, Joseph Vissarionovich Stalin was awarded the Order of Victory. It was conferred on him by the Presidium of the Supreme Soviet of the U.S.S.R. for his outstanding services in organizing and directing the offensive operations of the Red Army that resulted in the resounding defeat of the Germans and radically changed the situation in the war against the German-fascist invaders in favour of the Red Army.

The success of Stalin's strategical plan in 1944 was crowned by military and political results of first-rate importance. Under the blows of the Soviet forces, Rumania, Finland and Bulgaria surrendered and turned their arms against their former ally, Hitler Germany. Hungary was on the verge of capitulation. Germany was thus practically isolated. The resulting military situation meant that the Soviet Union was in a position, with her own forces alone and without the assistance of her allies, to occupy the whole of Germany and to liberate France. It was this circumstance that prompted the British Prime Minister, Winston Churchill, who until then had resisted the opening of a second front in Europe, to undertake an invasion of Western Europe. In June 1944, the Allies successfully effected a large-scale landing in Northern France.

Hitler Germany was now gripped in a vice between two fronts, as Comrade Stalin had foreseen she would be.

In his speech on November 6, 1944, on the occasion of the 27th anniversary of the Great October Socialist Revolution, Comrade Stalin expressed his confidence that the Red Army, having accomplished its patriotic task of liberating the Motherland, would fulfil its historical mission to the end, finish off the fascist beast in its own lair, and hoist the flag of victory over Berlin.

Stalin's summing up of the path traversed by the country and the army, and Stalin's call—On to Berlin!—were hailed by the Soviet people at the front and in the rear with profound enthusiasm.

The Soviet troops now launched the decisive offensive against the lair of the fascist beast. Very soon the Soviet Army had liberated Warsaw, the capital of Poland, from the Germans and penetrated into East Prussia. The Soviet armies developed their offensive along the whole front.

Early in February 1945, the leaders of the three Allied Powers—the U.S.S.R., the U.S.A. and Great Britain—met in conference in the Crimea.

Military and political decisions of first-rate importance were adopted at the conference on measures to encompass the final defeat of Germany and on her postwar status, as well as on the major political and economic problems of liberated Europe. The timing, scope and coordination of new and more powerful blows at Germany by the Allied armies from the East, West, North and South were agreed and planned in detail. At this conference, too, it was decided that the U.S.S.R. would enter the war against Japan.

The 27th anniversary of the Red Army, February 23, 1945, was celebrated by the Soviet Union amid outstanding historic victories. In January and February 1945, in a forty-day offensive the Soviet troops, by swift and skilful operations, had hurled the enemy far to the West, completely liberated Poland and a large part of Czechoslovakia and captured the major part of East Prussia and German Silesia. Under the Soviet assault, Hungary, Germany's last ally in Europe, dropped out of the war.

"Complete victory over the Germans is now already near,"* declared Comrade Stalin in his Order of the Day of February 23, 1945, summing up the successes of the Red Army's winter offensive.

He said that the Red Army had learned to crush and destroy the enemy according to all the rules of modern military science. "The generals and officers of the Red Army skilfully combine massed blows of powerful implements of war with skilful and swift manoeuvring."**

Operating in accordance with Stalin's strategical plan, the Red Army seized the major German strongholds in the South, captured Vienna, the capital of Austria, demolished the German army group cut off in East Prussia, seized the Silesian industrial area, which was of vital importance to Germany, and reached the approaches to Berlin. This cleared the way for the final and decisive assault on Hitler Germany.

Comrade Stalin's call "to hoist the flag of victory over Berlin"*** inspired the Soviet people to fresh feats of valour in labour and in the fields of battle.

On April 21, 1945, the eve of the assault of Berlin, J. V. Stalin, on behalf of the Soviet Govern-

---

* J. V. Stalin, *On the Great Patriotic War of the Soviet Union*, Moscow 1946, p. 185.

** *Ibid.,* p. 184.

*** *Ibid.,* p. 173.

ment, signed a Treaty of Friendship, Mutual Assistance and Postwar Collaboration between the U.S.S.R. and the Polish Republic. In his speech at this occasion, he said:

"The freedom-loving nations, and primarily the Slav nations, have been impatiently looking forward to the conclusion of this Treaty, for they realize that this Treaty signifies the consolidation of the united front of the United Nations against the common enemy in Europe."*

On May 2, 1945, the radio announced to the world an Order of the Day of the Supreme Commander-in-Chief to the Red Army and Navy declaring that the Soviet troops had "completed the defeat of the Berlin group of German troops and today, May 2, seized full possession of the capital of Germany, Berlin, the centre of German imperialism and the seat of German aggression."** The Red Army had obeyed Stalin's call: the flag of victory had been hoisted over Berlin!

The fate of Hitler Germany was sealed. On May 8, 1945, in Berlin, representatives of the German High Command signed an act of unconditional surrender of the armed forces of Germany. May 9 was proclaimed Victory Day, a national holiday in commemoration of the triumphant termination of

---

* *Ibid.*, p. 188.
** *Pravda*, No. 106, May 3, 1945.

the Great Patriotic War of the Soviet people, which had ended in the utter defeat of Hitler Germany.

On that historic day, Joseph Vissarionovich Stalin broadcasted an address to the people.

"Comrades! Fellow countrymen and countrywomen!

"The great day of victory over Germany has arrived. Fascist Germany, forced to her knees by the Red Army and the troops of our Allies, has admitted defeat and has announced her unconditional surrender....

"We now have full grounds for saying that the historic day of the final defeat of Germany, the day of our people's great victory over German imperialism, has arrived....

"Congratulations on our victory, my dear fellow countrymen and countrywomen!"*

When celebrating their victory, the thoughts and sentiments of the Soviet people were with him who had led our country through all the trials and tribulations of the war and had saved it from destruction, with him whose genius had mapped the road to victory and whose will had led the country to its triumph—with the great Stalin.

One of Comrade Stalin's major services to the country was that in the course of the Patriotic

* J. V. Stalin, *On the Great Patriotic War of the Soviet Union*, Moscow 1946, pp. 196-98.

War he selected, educated and promoted to positions of responsibility *new* military cadres, the men who bore the burden of the war against Germany and her allies: Bulganin, Vasilevsky, Konev, Govorov, Zhukov, Vatutin, Chernyakhovsky, Antonov, Sokolovsky, Meretskov, Rokossovsky, Malinovsky, Voronov, Tolbukhin, Yakovlev, Malinin, Galitsky, Trofimenko, Gorbatov, Shtemenko, Kurasov, Vershinin, Golovanov, Fedorenko, Rybalko, Bogdanov, Katukov, Lelyushenko and many others.

On May 24 the Soviet Government gave a reception in the Kremlin in honour of the commanders of the Red Army—commanders reared in the Stalin school.

Comrade Stalin spoke at the reception. He paid tribute to the Soviet people for its services in the Patriotic War, and primarily to the Russian people, as the most outstanding of all the nations that constitute the Soviet Union. The Russian people, he said, had earned universal recognition in the war as the leading force among the peoples of the Soviet Union. Comrade Stalin proposed a toast to the Russian people, not only because it was the leading people, but also because it was gifted with a clear mind, staunch character and patience. The boundless confidence of the Russian people in the Soviet Government, its faith in the correctness of the Government's policy and the unwavering support it gave the Government and the Bolshevik Party,

Stalin said, proved to be "the decisive factor which ensured our historic victory over the enemy of mankind, over fascism."*

On June 24, 1945, by order of Supreme Commander-in-Chief Stalin, a Victory Parade was held in Moscow of troops of the Army on active service, the Navy and the Moscow Garrison. To the Red Square the Soviet Army brought the standards of the German fascist armies and divisions it had vanquished and demolished. They were cast at the feet of the victorious Soviet people, at the foot of the Lenin Mausoleum, on the rostrum of which stood the Great Commander—Stalin.

The Presidium of the Supreme Soviet of the U.S.S.R., on June 26, 1945, expressing the will of the entire Soviet people, awarded a second Order of Victory to Marshal of the Soviet Union Joseph Vissarionovich Stalin for his outstanding services in organizing the armed forces of the Soviet Union and for his skilful leadership in the Great Patriotic War, which had ended with complete victory over Hitler Germany.

For having led the Red Army in the trying days of the defence of the country, and of its capital, Moscow, and for his exceptionally courageous and resolute direction of the fight against

---

* J. V. Stalin, *On the Great Patriotic War of the Soviet Union*, Moscow 1946, p. 201.

Hitler Germany, Marshal of the Soviet Union Joseph Vissarionovich Stalin was awarded the title of Hero of the Soviet Union, together with the Order of Lenin and the Gold Star medal that go with the title.

On June 27, 1945, Joseph Vissarionovich Stalin, Supreme Commander-in-Chief of the Armed Forces of the U.S.S.R., was invested with the highest military rank—Generalissimo of the Soviet Union.

On July 16, 1945, J. V. Stalin arrived in Berlin to attend the Tripartite Conference (July 17 to August 2), where the heads of the governments of the U.S.S.R., the U.S.A. and Great Britain adopted important decisions to consolidate the victory, including decisions on Germany, Austria and Poland.

Having triumphantly concluded the war against Hitler Germany, the Soviet Union turned its efforts to the formidable task of repairing the destruction caused by the German invaders, to rehabilitating its economy, to building new mills and factories.

But the Soviet Union could not consider itself secure as long as another hotbed of war still existed —in the shape of imperialist Japan, which had rejected the demand of the United States, Great Britain and China that she surrender unconditionally. The Allies proposed that the Soviet Government join the war against the Japanese aggressor. Loyal to its duty as an ally, the Soviet Government accepted the proposal and declared war on Japan.

The Soviet people endorsed and supported this decision of their government as the only way in which the security of the country could be safeguarded in the East, as well as in the West, as the only way in which the war could be ended and general peace re-established as speedily as possible.

On the morning of August 9, 1945, Soviet land forces and the Soviet Pacific Fleet opened hostilities against the Japanese in the Far East.

After desperate but unsuccessful counter-attacks, the Japanese Kwantung Army was forced to cease resistance, lay down its arms and surrender to the Soviet forces. The Soviet Army liberated from the Japanese Manchuria, South Sakhalin, Northern Korea, and the Kuril Islands.

The Soviet Union's entry into the war against Japan and the rout of large masses of Japanese troops as the result of the Soviet Army's impetuous offensive, compelled Japan to capitulate. On September 2, 1945, her political and military representatives signed an act of unconditional surrender in Tokyo.

On the day of the victory over Japan, Comrade Stalin addressed the Soviet people over the radio informing them of the glad tidings:

"Henceforth," he said, "we can regard our country as being free from the menace of German invasion in the West and of Japanese invasion in the East. The long-awaited peace for the peoples of all the world has come."*

This was a victory for the Soviet social system and the Soviet state system, for the Soviet armed forces and the wise policy of the Bolshevik Party.

During the years of the Patriotic War the Soviet people learned to appreciate even more fully the greatness of their leader, teacher, military commander and friend, Joseph Vissarionovich Stalin, his supreme devotion to the Soviet Motherland, and his constant concern for the progress and prosperity of the Socialist State.

It was Stalin that inspired the Soviet people to repulse the enemy, and it was he that led them to victory.

While directing the operations of the Soviet armed forces and the economic and organizational work in the rear, Comrade Stalin during the war continued his intense theoretical activity, developing and advancing the science of Marxism-Leninism.

In his wartime speeches and orders of the day (collected in the book, *On the Great Patriotic War of the Soviet Union*), the Soviet science of war, the theory of the Soviet socialist state, of its functions, and the sources of its strength received fur-

---

* J. V. Stalin, *On the Great Patriotic War of the Soviet Union*, Moscow 1946, p. 210.

ther development. He analyzed and drew general conclusions from the activities of the Soviet State under the conditions of war and indicated the way to strengthen its economic and military might.

In his speech on the occasion of the 26th anniversary of the Great October Socialist Revolution, Comrade Stalin showed how great had been the significance, in the effort to vanquish the fascist invaders, of the Bolshevik Party, the Soviet system, the friendship that bound together the nations of the Soviet Union, and the patriotism of the Soviet people.

"In this Patriotic War the Party has been the inspirer and organizer of the nation-wide struggle against the fascist invaders. The organizational work conducted by our Party has united all the efforts of the Soviet people, directing them towards the common goal, and concentrating all our strength and resources on the task of defeating the enemy. In the course of the war the Party has still further strengthened its bonds of kinship with the people, it has become still more closely connected with the masses of the working people.

"This is one of the sources of the strength of our state."*

---

* J. V. Stalin, *On the Great Patriotic War of the Soviet Union,* Moscow 1946, p. 123.

Generalissimo of the Soviet Union J. V. Stalin with a group of marshals, generals and admirals—deputies of the Supreme Soviet of the U.S.S.R.

Photo

Another source of strength of the Soviet Union was the Soviet socialist system.

"The experience of the war has proved that the Soviet system is not only the best system for organizing the economic and cultural development of a country in the period of peaceful construction, but also the best system for mobilizing all the forces of the people to resist an enemy in wartime."*

"The socialist system which was engendered by the October Revolution imbued our people and our army with great and invincible strength."**

The war was a stern test of all the material and moral forces of the Soviet State, a test of its stability and virility. The Soviet Socialist State emerged with credit from the test of war, stronger and more stable than ever, as Comrade Stalin had foreseen it would.

Generalizing the experience of the war, Stalin drew new conclusions relative to the value and importance of the Soviet economic system. The war, he said, had proved that "the economic basis of the Soviet State is immeasurably more virile than the economies of the enemy countries."***

Whereas the economies of the enemy countries

---

* *Ibid.*, p. 123.
** *Ibid.*, p. 163.
*** *Ibid.*

had fallen into decline during the war, the Soviet Union was able not only to supply the front with sufficient quantities of arms and ammunition, but also to accumulate reserves. In the last three years of the war the Soviet tank industry annually produced an average of over 30,000 tanks, self-propelled guns and armoured cars; the aircraft industry nearly 40,000 aeroplanes; the ordnance industry nearly 120,000 guns of all calibres, 450,000 light and heavy machine guns, over 3,000,000 rifles and about 2,000,000 tommy guns, and the mortar industry up to 100,000 mortars. The quality of Soviet armaments was not only not inferior, but even superior to the German.

Appraising the role played by the Soviet people in the fight against the German fascist invaders, Comrade Stalin drew the highly significant conclusion that they had rendered a supreme service to mankind. "By their self-sacrificing struggle the Soviet people saved the civilization of Europe from the fascist pogrom-mongers."*

He appraised the Soviet people as a heroic people, capable of performing miracles and emerging victorious from the most gruelling tests.

Another major source of strength of the Soviet Union, Comrade Stalin pointed out, was the mutual

---

* J. V. Stalin, *On the Great Patriotic War of the Soviet Union,* Moscow 1946, p. 167.

friendship of the peoples of our country, which had withstood all the trials and hardships of the war against the fascist invaders and emerged more steeled and tempered than ever. The great and indestructible friendship of the peoples of our country is anchored in the firm foundation of Lenin's and Stalin's national policy, and is a model of an equitable solution of the national problem without precedent in history.

The Hitlerite ideology of bestial nationalism and race hatred was vanquished by the Soviet ideology of the equality of all races and nations, the ideology of friendship among peoples. The Soviet people not only scored a military and economic victory over Hitler Germany, but inflicted on her moral and political defeat.

Of supreme importance are Stalin's views on Soviet patriotism, as a source of the labour heroism of the Soviet people in the rear and of the martial heroism of the Soviet soldiers at the front. "The strength of Soviet patriotism lies in the fact that it is based not on racial or nationalistic prejudices, but on the profound devotion and loyalty of the people to their Soviet Motherland, on the fraternal cooperation of the working people of all the nations inhabiting our country. Soviet patriotism is a harmonious blend of the national traditions of the peoples and the common vital interests of all the working people of the Soviet Union.... At the same time, the peoples of the U.S.S.R. respect the rights and independence of the peoples of foreign countries and have always shown their readiness to live in peace and friendship with neighbouring countries. This should be regarded as the basis upon which the ties between our country and other freedom-loving peoples are expanding and growing stronger."*

The advanced Soviet science of war received further development at Comrade Stalin's hands. He elaborated the theory of the permanently operating factors that decide the issue of wars, of active defence and the laws of counter-offensive and offensive, of the cooperation of all services and arms in modern warfare, of the role of big tank masses and air forces in modern war, and of the artillery as the most formidable of the armed services. At the various stages of the war Stalin's genius found the correct solutions, that took account of all the circumstances of the situation.

His strategical mastership was displayed both in defence and offence. At his orders, the Soviet forces combined active defence with preparations for counter-offensive operations, and offensive operations with effective defence. He skilfully elaborated and applied new tactics of manoeuvring—

---

* J. V. Stalin, *On the Great Patriotic War of the Soviet Union*, Moscow 1946, p. 165.

the tactics of piercing the enemy's front in several sectors simultaneously, so as not to allow him to collect his reserves into a striking force, the tactics of piercing the enemy's front on several sectors in succession, so as to compel him to lose time and effort in regrouping his forces, and the tactics of piercing the enemy's flanks, outflanking him, surrounding and annihilating large enemy army groups. His genius enabled him to divine the enemy's plans and defeat them. The battles in which Comrade Stalin directed the Soviet armies are brilliant examples of operational skill.

All the operations carried out by the Soviet Army under the command of Generalissimo Stalin bear the stamp of unique creative thought and originality.

Comrade Stalin's solutions of the problems of international relations and Soviet foreign policy both during and after the war are exemplary instances of the scientific approach. He outlined a concrete, practical program of action and policy for the organization and reconstruction of the political, economic and cultural life of the European nations after the victory over fascist Germany.

At the height of the war, in 1942, he formulated the major principles of the program of the anti-Hitler coalition: abolition of racial exclusiveness; equality of nations and inviolability of their territories; liberation of the enslaved nations and restoration of their sovereign rights; the right of every nation to manage its affairs in its own way; restoration of the democratic liberties.

In his speech on the occasion of the 27th anniversary of the Great October Socialist Revolution, Comrade Stalin said: "To win the war against Germany means consummating a great historical cause. But winning the war does not yet mean ensuring the peoples a durable peace and reliable security in the future. The task is not only to win the war, but also to prevent the outbreak of fresh aggression and another war, if not for ever, then at least for a long time to come."*

Speaking of the necessity of ensuring world-wide security and creating an international organization, Comrade Stalin warned that the measures taken in this direction by the United Nations "will be effective if the Great Powers who have borne the brunt of the war against Hitler Germany continue to act in a spirit of unanimity and harmony. They will not be effective if this essential condition is violated."**

A majestic picture of the historic victories won by the Soviet Union in the Patriotic War, and an

---

* J. V. Stalin, *On the Great Patriotic War of the Soviet Union*, Moscow 1946, pp. 170-71.
** *Ibid.*, p. 173.

imposing program for the further development of the forces of Socialist society were sketched by Comrade Stalin in his speech to the meeting of voters in the Stalin Electoral District, Moscow, on February 9, 1946. He spoke of the new, fourth, five-year plan of economic development, the main objective of which was to recover and then to exceed the prewar level of industrial and agricultural output.

He spoke of the plans for the future, for the further powerful progress of the economy of the Soviet Union and its science, and the creation of conditions which would guarantee our country against all contingencies, increase its economic and military might and ensure the continued cultural progress and growing prosperity of its people.

In February 1946 new elections were held to the Supreme Soviet of the U.S.S.R. on the basis of the Stalin Constitution. The elections were an eloquent and convincing demonstration of the loyalty of the Soviet people to the Bolshevik Party, to the Soviet Government, and to their beloved Stalin. The candidates of the Communist and non-Party bloc received 99.18 per cent of the vote to the Soviet of the Union, and 99.16 per cent of the vote to the Soviet of Nationalities.

* * *

Comrade Stalin's life and activities are inseparably bound up with the activities of Lenin, his teacher and preceptor, with the history of the heroic Bolshevik Party and the history of the great Soviet people.

His life and activities are linked with the international working-class movement and the struggle for national emancipation of the colonial peoples from the imperialist yoke. The Communist International grew and developed under the guidance of the great leaders, Lenin and Stalin. Just as the history of the First International is inseparably associated with the names of Marx and Engels, so the history of the Third, Communist International is associated with the names of Lenin and Stalin. The Communist International played a big role in welding the vanguard of the politically advanced workers into genuine working-class parties. Having fulfilled its historical mission, the Communist International terminated its existence during the second world war. In May 1943, the Presidium of the Executive Committee of the Communist International decided to recommend the dissolution of the Comintern as a directing centre of the international working-class movement. The proposal was endorsed by the national sections of the International.

Millions of workers in all countries look upon Stalin as their teacher, from whose classic writings they learn how to cope with the class enemy and how to pave the way for the ultimate victory of the proletariat. Stalin's influence is the influence of the great and glorious Bolshevik Party, to which workers in the capitalist countries look as a model to follow, a model of what a working-class party should be. It was under the leadership of this Party that capitalism was overthrown and the power of the Soviets, the power of the working people, established, and under its leadership that Socialism was built in the U.S.S.R.

The workers of all countries know that every word pronounced by Stalin is the word of the Soviet people, and that his every word is backed by the deed. The triumph of the Socialist Revolution, the building of Socialism in the U.S.S.R., and the victory of the Soviet people in their Patriotic War have convinced the labouring masses of the world of the deep and vital truth of the cause of Lenin and Stalin. And today all freedom-loving peoples look upon Stalin as a loyal and staunch champion of peace and security and of the democratic liberties.

J. V. Stalin is the genius, the leader and teacher of the Party, the great strategist of Socialist revolution, helmsman of the Soviet State and captain of armies. An implacable attitude towards the enemies of Socialism, profound fidelity to principle, a combination of clear revolutionary perspective and clarity of purpose with extraordinary firmness and persistence in the pursuit of aims, wise and practical leadership, and constant contact with the masses—such are the characteristic features of Stalin's style. After Lenin, no other leader in the world has been called upon to direct such vast masses of workers and peasants as J. V. Stalin. He has a unique faculty for generalizing the creative revolutionary experience of the masses, for seizing upon and developing their initiative, for learning from the masses as well as teaching them, and for leading them forward to victory.

Stalin's whole work is an example of profound theoretical power combined with an unusual breadth and versatility of practical experience in the revolutionary struggle.

In conjunction with the tried and tested Leninists who are his immediate associates, and at the head of the great Bolshevik Party, Stalin guides the destinies of a multinational Socialist State, a state of workers and peasants of which there is no precedent in history. His advice is a guide to action in all fields of Socialist construction. His work is extraordinary for its variety; his energy truly amazing. The range of questions which engage his attention is immense, embracing the most complex problems of Marxist-Leninist theory and school textbooks; problems of Soviet foreign policy and the municipal affairs of the proletarian capital; the development of the Great Northern Sea Route and the reclamation of the Colchian marshes; the advancement of Soviet literature and art and the editing of the model rules for collective farms; and, lastly, the solution of most intricate problems in the theory and practice of war.

Everybody is familiar with the cogent and invincible force of Stalin's logic, the crystal clarity of his mind, his iron will, his devotion to the Party, his ardent faith in the people, and love for the people. Everybody is familiar with his modesty, his simplicity of manner, his consideration for people, and his merciless severity towards enemies of the people. Everybody is familiar with his intolerance of ostentation, of phrasemongers and windbags, of whiners and alarmists. Stalin is wise and deliberate in solving complex political questions where a thorough weighing of pros and cons is required. At the same time, he is a supreme master of bold revolutionary decisions and of swift realignments.

Stalin is the worthy continuer of the cause of Lenin, or, as it is said in the Party: Stalin is the Lenin of today.

Replying to the congratulations of public bodies and individuals on his fiftieth birthday, in 1929, Stalin wrote: "I set down your congratulations and greetings as addressed to the great Party of the working class, which begot me and reared me in its image. . . .

"You need have no doubt, comrades, that I am prepared in the future, too, to devote to the cause of the working class, to the cause of the proletarian revolution and world Communism, all my strength, all my faculties, and, if need be, all my blood, to the very last drop."*

In the eyes of the peoples of the U.S.S.R., Stalin is the incarnation of their heroism, their love of their country, their patriotism. "For Stalin! For our country!"—it was with this cry that the valiant Soviet Army demolished its malignant and treacherous enemy, fascist Germany, and hoisted the flag of victory over Berlin.

"For Stalin! For our country!"—it was with this cry that the men of the Soviet Army and Navy demolished imperialist Japan and brought security to the frontiers of the Soviet Union in the Far East.

With the name of Stalin in their hearts, the working class of the Soviet Union performed unparalleled feats of labour in the Great Patriotic War, supplying the Red Army with first-class weapons and ammunition.

With the name of Stalin in their hearts, the collective farmers toiled devotedly in the fields to supply the Red Army and the cities with food, and industry with raw materials.

---

* J. V. Stalin, *Collected Works*, Russ. ed., Vol. 12, p. 140.

With the name of Stalin in their hearts, the Soviet intelligentsia worked with might and main in defence of their country, perfecting the weapons of the Red Army and the technique and organization of industry, and furthering Soviet science and culture.

With the name of Stalin in their hearts, the entire Soviet people are now successfully repairing the damage caused by the war and are striving for a new powerful advance of the Soviet national economy and Soviet culture.

Stalin's name is a symbol of the courage and glory of the Soviet people, a call to heroic deeds for the welfare of their great Motherland.

Stalin's name is cherished by the boys and girls of the Socialist Land, by the Young Pioneers. Their dearest ambition is to be like Lenin and Stalin, to be political figures of the Lenin and Stalin type. At the call of the Party and Comrade Stalin, the youth of the Soviet Union have erected giant socialist industrial plants, have reared cities in the taiga, have built splendid ships, are conquering the Arctic, are mastering new methods in industry and agriculture, are strengthening the defences of our Motherland, are working creatively in the sciences and the arts. At the call of the Party and Stalin, they displayed exemplary heroism and courage in the battlefields of the Patriotic War and exemplary devotion in the rear, working for the victory of the Red Army. Fostered by Lenin and Stalin, the Young Communist League is a true aid of the Bolshevik Party, a reliable successor to the older generation of fighters for Communism.

In all their many languages the peoples of the Soviet Union compose songs to Stalin, expressing their supreme love and boundless devotion for their great leader, teacher, friend and military commander.

In the lore and art of the people, Stalin's name is ever linked with Lenin's. "We go with Stalin as with Lenin, we talk to Stalin as to Lenin; he knows all our inmost thoughts; all his life he has cared for us," runs one of the many exquisite Russian folk tales of today.

The name of Stalin is a symbol of the moral and political unity of Soviet society.

With the name of Stalin, all progressive men and women, all the freedom-loving democratic peoples associate their hope for lasting peace and security.

"It is our good fortune that in the trying years of the war the Red Army and the Soviet people were led forward by the wise and tested leader of the Soviet Union—the Great Stalin. With the name of Generalissimo Stalin the glorious victories of our army will go down in the history of our country and in the history of the world. Under the guidance of Stalin, the great leader and organizer, we are now proceeding to peaceful constructive labours, striving to bring the forces of Socialist society to full fruition and to justify the dearest hopes of our friends all over the world."*

* V. M. Molotov, *Speech on the 28th Anniversary of the Great October Socialist Revolution*, Russ. ed., 1945, pp. 18-19.

★

Printed in the United Kingdom
by Lightning Source UK Ltd.
117890UK00001B/13